HOW TO MAKE GLUTEN FREE BREAD THAT ACTUALLY TASTES GOOD

CELESTE NOLAND

HOW TO MAKE GLUTEN FREE BREAD THAT ACTUALLY TASTES GOOD BY CELESTE NOLAND

PUBLISHED BY CELESTE NOLAND, LIFE AFTER WHEAT LLC

HTTPS://THEREISLIFEAFTERWHEAT.COM

BOOK DESIGN BY MICHAELA BRADY
PHOTOGRAPHY BY CELESTE NOLAND
COVER IMAGE © CELESTE NOLAND

ISBN: 9798787974447

FIRST EDITION

TO MY MOM, WHO PATIENTLY ALLOWED MANY A MESS AS I EXPERIMENTED IN THE KITCHEN; AND TO ALLAN, WHO IS THE REASON I BEGAN CREATING AND SHARING RECIPES, AND CONTINUES TO BE MY INSPIRATION AND BIGGEST SUPPORT.

WELCOME!

I'm Celeste, the owner of Life After Wheat at https://thereislifeafterwheat.com. I have always loved spending time in the kitchen, and over the past 8 years have been perfecting the art of gluten free baking and cooking.

When my husband was diagnosed with multiple food allergies, I was so disappointed by the options and didn't want him to miss out. Although there are a lot more options now, I know that so many of you feel the same way and wish that you could enjoy your favorites again.

Whenever I talk to someone who is just starting to eat gluten free, the first question is always what to do for bread. Bread is such a staple, and it really is tough to find a good gluten free bread. It took me a long time, but the first recipe I developed was gluten free bread. Something that is soft and bendable, has that slightly sweet and hearty homemade flavor, and is so good fresh out of the oven that you just can't resist having an extra slice. Bread making is an art, and baking gluten free bread is a different experience entirely. That's why I created step-by-step instructions with each of the recipes you'll find in this book.

I love helping people discover just how good gluten free food can taste by sharing my family's favorite recipes and products!

–CELESTE

CONTENTS

THEREISLIFEAFTERWHEAT.COM

CONTENTS

KITCHEN TOOLS I RECOMMEND

- KitchenAid mixer (with paddle attachment)
- Dough scraper
- Good spatula
- Pie bag
- Parchment and/or baking mats
- Loaf pans
- Sheet pans
- Hamburger pan
- Hoagie pan
- Oven thermometer
- Instant read thermometer

Find links to all of these items at https://thereislifeafterwheat.com/cookbook

INGREDIENTS YOU'LL NEED

FLOUR

- gfJules flour OR ingredients to make your own flour blend (see page xv)

YEAST

- Not all yeasts are gluten free, so be sure to check labels! I usually use SAF brand instant yeast. If you choose to use a regular yeast instead of instant, be aware that you'll need to allow for more rising time.
- There is no need to proof the yeast, just add it in with your dry ingredients.
- Store yeast in a cool, dry location. If you don't use it often, store it in the refrigerator and pull it out at least 30 minutes prior to using it, to allow it to come to room temperature.
- If your yeast is not fresh enough, it won't provide a good rise. To test your yeast, proof it by adding 1 teaspoon of sugar and 2 1/4 teaspoons of yeast to 1/4 cup of warm water. Wait 10 minutes, and if the mixture bubbles, increases in size, and develops a yeasty aroma, then it is still good.

INGREDIENTS YOU'LL NEED

INSTANT MILK POWDER

- I use instant milk powder in almost all gluten free bread and roll recipes for 2 reasons:
1. It provides a richer flavor
2. It helps with browning. Gluten free baked goods often don't brown as well, and the dairy helps to provide a beautiful crust.
- You can use any brand of instant milk powder (also called powdered milk), but always check the label to be sure it is gluten free. I typically order Anthony's brand from Amazon.
- If you need a dairy free option, you can use Native Forest coconut milk powder.

EGGS AND BUTTER

- For best results, bring eggs and butter to room temperature before mixing the dough. If you're pressed for time, set the eggs in a bowl of warm (not hot) water for 5-10 minutes, and soften butter for 5-15 seconds in the microwave.
- Using a low-fat butter alternative such as margarine is not recommended.
- See page xix for dairy and egg substitutions.

INGREDIENTS YOU'LL NEED

SUGAR
- All my recipes call for at least a little sugar. This is because yeast needs sugar in order to activate and give rise to your baked goods. In some recipes, such as the sandwich bread, you can substitute honey instead if you prefer.
- Do not omit the sugar from any recipe.

SALT
- If you are on a low sodium diet, feel free to reduce the salt in any recipe as needed. While it will obviously affect the flavor, I often reduce the salt because two of my kids have to watch their intake.

WATER
- Always use water that is just above room temperature. Using cold water will inhibit the activation of yeast. Water that is too hot can kill the yeast. Water should be 105-110°F.

Find links to all of these items at https://thereislifeafterwheat.com/cookbook

HOW TO

MEASURING FLOUR

When baking, it is always important to use the correct amount of flour; this is especially true with *gluten free* baking, because if you use too much flour, you'll end up with gritty, dry, or crumbly baked goods. When measuring flour, always follow these steps:

1: STIR FLOUR.
2: WITH A SPOON, SCOOP FLOUR INTO MEASURING CUP UNTIL IT IS HEAPED ABOVE THE RIM.
3: LEVEL OFF THE TOP WITH THE HANDLE OF THE SPOON OR THE FLAT EDGE OF A BUTTER KNIFE.

THEREISLIFEAFTERWHEAT.COM

HOW TO

TEXTURE OF DOUGH

Gluten free flours soak up more moisture when baking than their wheat counterparts, so in order to get that soft-and-fluffy texture, you'll need to start with a dough that is wet and sticky.

The texture should be between a thick banana bread batter and a regular wheat-based dough: it should not form a ball as it is mixed, should be too sticky to handle with bare hands, but definitely be considered a dough as opposed to a batter.

NOTE: I live at around 4,000 feet, which means that if you are at a much lower altitude, you might need to make a few adjustments to your dough such as allowing for a slower rise time, or possibly adding additional water or flour if the dough isn't the right texture. (See photo below.)

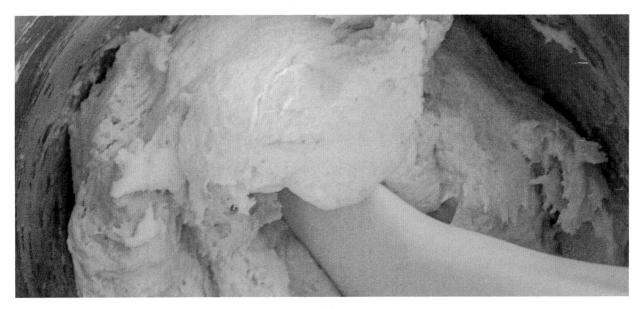

HOW TO

HANDLING DOUGH (FLOUR, OIL)

Some people assume that because gluten free dough is sticky, it needs to simply fill the pan that it is in. But there are ways to make all the fun shapes of breads and rolls you love! Here are two methods I use often:

1: FLOUR

This is the method I prefer and use most often. It involves coating the dough in enough flour to enable shaping, but not working the flour *into* the dough. You'll dust your surface with a tablespoon or two of flour, turn the dough out onto the floured surface, then roll it gently to coat the entire surface. Keep some flour nearby in case you need more flour as you go.

2: OIL/BUTTER

I use this method with my cloverleaf rolls which you can find on page 59. It can be a way to add flavor (add garlic salt or other seasonings), additional moisture, or just avoid sticking. Put a couple tablespoons of oil or melted butter in a small bowl, coat your hands and surface and apply more as needed. A word of caution: only use as much as needed and don't add too much oil or it will affect the texture.

FLOUR

You might have noticed that gluten free flour isn't just one ingredient, but is made up of a blend of flours, starches, and usually a binding agent such as xanthan gum.

This is because there is no direct substitute for wheat flour that will yield the same results. If you use a straight swap of rice flour in a recipe, for instance, you will end up with a very dry and crumbly baked good that didn't really rise and, quite frankly, doesn't taste good.

Sometimes, the sheer number of gluten free flour blends on the market can be overwhelming (and expensive!). That's why for this cookbook, I have kept it simple for you and tested every recipe with just two flour blend options: a purchased option called gfJules, and my homemade flour blend recipe.

You can choose which option works best for you based on ingredients and cost, and don't have to experiment with lots of different types.

Over the years, I have tried a lot of different flour blends for breads and rolls and gfJules outperforms all the rest every time. It just yields a lighter, fluffier bread product.

HOMEMADE FLOUR BLEND RECIPE

- 1 cup white rice flour
- 2 cup brown rice flour, sorghum flour, or a combination of the two (I usually use half and half)
- 1 1/3 cup potato starch
- 1 1/3 cup tapioca starch
- 6 tsp xanthan gum

1. Whisk all ingredients together by hand or with your KitchenAid whisk attachment.
2. Store in an airtight container in a cool location (does not require refrigeration). Use within 1 month.
3. This blend works best for yeast breads/rolls and quick breads/muffins. It is not recommended for cookies.

HOW TO

KNEADING/RISING

Here's a silver lining: making gluten free yeast breads/rolls takes roughly half the time it would take to make the regular wheat version. Why? Because there is no gluten, kneading the dough doesn't provide any benefit (kneading is a step that helps to activate the gluten) and the dough actually performs better with only one rise. Here's what you'll do instead:

Skip the kneading. You'll notice my recipes *never* call for kneading. You'll measure the ingredients, use a stand mixer to form the dough (or hand mixer if you don't have one, but I highly recommend investing in a stand mixer), skip the first rise and go straight to shaping, rise once, then bake.

HOW TO

LET'S TALK ABOUT GLUTEN

Gluten is the binding agent in regular flour that holds your baked goods together. Gluten free flours do not, obviously, contain gluten so they are prone to being crumbly and dry if you don't add some sort of binding agent.

Most gluten free products have either xanthan gum or guar gum to accomplish this. I've used both, and have found that while xanthan gum is a little (not a lot) more expensive than guar gum, it does a better job while using less in your recipes.

Adding a binder isn't optional for gluten free baking recipes, and all my recipes use xanthan gum because I have found it yields better results in bread products.

HOW TO

HOW/WHERE TO RISE
- Use proof setting on oven.
- Preheat oven to 100°F, then turn off and place dough inside with the door closed.
- Preheat oven and let rise on top of oven.

COOLING
- In pan for 10 minutes.
- Cool completely on rack before slicing.

STORING/REHEATING
- Any homemade bread product without added preservatives will become crumbly over a few days' time. Gluten free products tend to do so a little quicker and are best served just after they have fully cooled. I'll provide storage instructions at the end of each recipe, but as a general rule allow your baked goods to cool **completely**, then place in a freezer bag, press out all the air, seal, and store in the freezer. You might want to slice before you freeze so it is easy to pull out as much as you need.
- To reheat, warm in the microwave, or pop bread in the toaster.

HOW TO

DAIRY FREE/EGG FREE SUBSTITUTIONS

- **Most of my recipes can be made egg and/or dairy free very easily.**
  - **Bob's Red Mill egg replacer** has worked very well for me, my family couldn't tell the difference when I used it for my sandwich bread recipe (page 4).
- If you need to make a recipe dairy free, follow these substitution guidelines:
  - **Butter**: Use butter substitute that is in stick form, not a tub.
  - **Instant milk powder**: I use instant milk powder in almost every recipe because it yields a richer flavor and helps with browning. I recommend using coconut milk powder as a dairy free substitute.

TROUBLE-SHOOTING

PROBLEM	SOLUTION
Soggy on the bottom	left to cool in pan too long, too much butter when greasing pan
Didn't rise well	too much flour, wrong type of flour, yeast not fresh, environment too cool
Fell after baking	didn't bake long enough, not enough flour
Dough is sticking to my hands	coat with more flour, oil hands
Stuck to surface	better grease pan, use parchment paper or baking mat

FREQUENTLY ASKED QUESTIONS

I don't have a stand mixer, can I still make these recipes?

The short answer is yes, you can. That being said, I consider a stand mixer to be a very worthwhile investment if you're going to be making your own gluten free baked goods because it will be easier and yield the best results. I have had my KitchenAid stand mixer for almost 10 years now and consider it my favorite kitchen appliance!

I don't have gfJules gluten free flour, and I don't want to make my own. Can I use what I have on hand?

No. I have tested these recipes with many gluten free flour blends and I promise the results are worth the price and/or effort! If you cannot tolerate corn and truly don't want to make your own gluten free flour blend, you can use Better Batter brand, but be aware that you won't get quite the same rise.

I can't tolerate xanthan gum, can I leave it out of the homemade flour blend or substitute with something else?

Xanthan gum is what creates the same binding structure as gluten in gluten free products. I haven't tested these recipes with any alternative, and the xanthan gum is crucial for texture and rise.

Can I use a bread machine for these recipes?

I haven't tested any of these recipes in a bread machine. I find that gluten free bread is so easy with only one rise and no kneading required, that it isn't worth it for me to research and purchase a bread machine.

THEREISLIFEAFTERWHEAT.COM

FREQUENTLY ASKED QUESTIONS

I don't eat sugar, can I omit it or use a sugar substitute in your recipes?

Yeast requires a little sugar in order to create a good rise, so you cannot omit it entirely. For savory breads that don't require much sugar, you can substitute honey if you would like, but I haven't tested any of these recipes with coconut sugar or sugar substitutes.

I am on a low sodium diet, can I omit or reduce the sodium in these recipes?

I have two kids who are also on low sodium diets, so I can relate! We often halve the salt called for in the recipe and have great results.

Do I have to use *instant* yeast, or can I just use regular yeast?

I prefer to use instant yeast because it cuts down on rise time and doesn't require proofing with water/sugar before adding to the recipe. If you choose to use regular instead of instant, go ahead and stir together the yeast, warm water, and sugar and allow it to get nice and bubbly before adding to the remaining ingredients and mixing.

Can I omit the oil/butter in these recipes, or substitute applesauce?

I don't recommend omitting or substituting the fat in any of these recipes. If you are on a limited fat diet, there are several recipes in this cookbook with small amounts of butter/oil such as the Sandwich Bread and French Herb Mini Loaves.

SAVORY BREADS

BAKING TIP

DID YOU KNOW THAT RICE-BASED FLOURS DON'T BROWN AS WELL IN THE OVEN AS WHEAT FLOUR? ADDING INSTANT MILK POWDER ADDS A RICHER FLAVOR AND HELPS YOUR BREAD TAKE ON A GOLDEN BROWN COLOR WHILE BAKING.

SANDWICH BREAD

YIELD: 1 LOAF PREP: 15M COOK: 45M TOTAL TIME: 2HRS

A classic and easy recipe for soft, bendable sandwich bread based on my husband's grandma's recipe.

INGREDIENTS

- 3 cups gluten free flour
- 1 tablespoon instant yeast
- 2 tablespoons gluten free potato flakes (instant potatoes)
- 1 teaspoon salt
- 1/2 cup instant milk powder (see notes for dairy free)
- 2 tablespoons sugar or honey
- 1 large egg, room temp
- 1 3/4 cup warm water, slightly warmer than room temp
- 1 tablespoon butter, softened (see notes for dairy free)

RECIPE NOTES

- If you can't tolerate potatoes or don't have instant potato flakes on hand, feel free to omit them.
- I know it's hard, but the texture will be much better if you let the bread cool completely before slicing.
- For dairy free, use a butter substitute in stick form, not the tub.

SANDWICH BREAD

INSTRUCTIONS

1. Add all ingredients to the bowl of a stand mixer in order listed.
2. Mix on medium speed for 3 minutes. The texture should be between a thick banana bread batter and a regular wheat-based dough (**see page xii**). and additional water or flour 1 tablespoon at a time if needed to attain this consistency.
3. Grease bottom and corners of a loaf pan. I use butter.
4. Spread batter in loaf pan, peaking the middle a bit lengthwise instead of spreading flat.
5. Cover lightly with plastic wrap sprayed with cooking spray or oil and let rise in a warm place until loaf has almost doubled in size. I use the rapid proof option on my oven and it takes about 25 minutes.
6. Preheat to 350°F.
7. Bake for 45-50 minutes, until the bread is a nice deep golden brown on top and reaches at least 190°F. If you take it out too early, it will fall as it is cooling.
8. Brush the top with butter.
9. Let cool for 10 minutes in the pan before removing to the wire rack.
10. Let cool completely before slicing.
11. Be sure to enjoy it fresh! It is best this way.
12. The best way to store gluten free bread is to slice, place in a Ziploc freezer bag, remove all the air, seal, and freeze. You can then remove a slice and pop it in the toaster or microwave as you need. It might help to put pieces of wax or parchment paper between the slices so they don't stick together.
13. Once you have frozen the bread, it's best toasted or warmed in the microwave for 10-15 seconds. I don't recommend refrigeration as the bread tends to crumble easily.

BAKING TIP

DON'T CUT THE SUGAR!
YEAST REQUIRES A
LITTLE SUGAR IN ORDER
TO ACTIVATE, SO IF
YOU'RE TRYING TO CUT
SUGAR, BE SURE TO USE
AT LEAST THE SAME
AMOUNT OF SUGAR AS
YEAST CALLED FOR IN
YOUR RECIPE.

PEASANT BREAD

⊕ YIELD: 1 LOAF   ⊙ PREP: 10M   ⧗ COOK: 30M   ⊙ TOTAL TIME: 2HRS

A simple, comforting, homestyle loaf of bread that is beautifully soft and ridiculously easy to make.

INGREDIENTS

- 2 cups + 2 tablespoons gluten free flour
- 3/4 teaspoon salt
- 1 tablespoon sugar
- 1 1/2 teaspoons instant yeast
- 1/3 cup instant milk powder
- 1 1/3 cups warm water, slightly warmer than room temp
- 1 tablespoon butter, softened plus more for greasing bowl

RECIPE NOTES

- Feel free to double this recipe and make 2 loaves.
- I love serving this as a side with soup!

THEREISLIFEAFTERWHEAT.COM

PEASANT BREAD

INSTRUCTIONS

1. Generously grease a 1 quart oven-safe bowl with butter (I use Pyrex brand)
2. Add all ingredients to the bowl of a stand mixer in order listed.
3. Mix on medium speed for 3 minutes. The texture should be between a thick banana bread batter and a regular wheat-based dough (**see page xii**).
4. Turn out onto a floured surface and turn to coat, gently shaping into a round loaf.
5. Transfer the ball of dough to the prepared bowl and cover loosely with plastic wrap.
6. Allow to rise in a warm place for 30-45 minutes until doubled in size.
7. Preheat the oven to 425°F.
8. Bake for 15 minutes, then with the bread still in the oven and the oven door closed, reduce heat to 375°F and bake for another 15-20 minutes until the bread is a light golden brown on top and internal temperature is 190°F.
9. Allow the bread to cool for 10 minutes in the bowl before removing to a cooling rack.
10. Cool completely before slicing.
11. This bread tastes so good with a bowl of soup or chili! It's also great for sandwiches, French toast, or anything else you would do with a good slice of bread.

BAKING TIP

TOO MUCH FLOUR = DRY AND CRUMBLY BREAD. TO AVOID THIS, ALWAYS FOLLOW THESE STEPS WHEN MEASURING GLUTEN FREE FLOUR:

1. STIR THE FLOUR WITH A SPOON OR WHISK.
2. USING A SPOON, SCOOP FLOUR INTO A MEASURING CUP UNTIL IT IS HEAPING ABOVE THE RIM. BE CAREFUL NOT TO PACK THE FLOUR!
3. LEVEL THE FLOUR WITH THE FLAT EDGE OF A TABLE KNIFE.

CHEESY BREAD

YIELD: 1 LOAF   PREP: 15M   COOK: 50M   TOTAL TIME: 2HRS

A hearty bread packed with flavor! Tastes great fresh out of the oven and also makes a delicious sandwich.

INGREDIENTS

- 3 cups gluten free flour (gfJules)
- 3 tablespoons sugar
- 1 tablespoon yeast
- 1 teaspoon salt
- 1/3 cup instant milk powder
- 1 teaspoon baking powder
- 1 large egg, room temp
- 3/4 cup sour cream OR plain Greek yogurt
- 1 1/4 cups warm water, slightly warmer than room temp
- 1 cup grated cheddar cheese (sharp or medium work best)

RECIPE NOTES

- Try experimenting with different cheese! While I usually make this loaf with a medium or sharp cheddar, you can use mild cheddar, colby jack, pepper jack, or any other of your favorite hard cheeses.
- My husband loves using the leftovers for sandwiches, either a double-grilled cheese or a lunch meat sandwich with the bread toasted.

THEREISLIFEAFTERWHEAT.COM

CHEESY BREAD

INSTRUCTIONS

1. Grease a loaf pan with butter. Set aside.
2. Combine all ingredients *except grated cheese* in a stand mixer and mix for 2 minutes on medium speed. The texture should be between a thick banana bread batter and a regular wheat-based dough (**see page xii**).
3. Add grated cheese and mix just until combined.
4. Turn out onto a floured surface and turn to coat, gently shaping into a loaf.
5. Carefully place loaf into the prepared pan and cover loosely with plastic wrap.
6. Allow to rise in a warm place for about 30 minutes or until almost doubled in size.
7. Preheat oven to 350°F and bake for 50 minutes, until the loaf is a golden brown color.
8. Allow bread to cool in pan for 10 minutes, then transfer to a cooling rack.
9. Cool completely before slicing.
10. Be sure to enjoy it fresh! It is best this way.
11. The best way to store gluten free bread is to slice, place in a Ziploc freezer bag, remove all the air, seal, and freeze. You can then remove a slice and pop it in the toaster or microwave as you need. It might help to put pieces of wax or parchment paper between the slices so they don't stick together.
12. Once you have frozen the bread, it's best toasted or warmed in the microwave for 10-15 seconds. I don't recommend refrigeration as the bread tends to crumble easily.

BAKING TIP

ALTITUDE AFFECTS ANY TYPE OF BAKING. ALL OF THE RECIPES IN THIS BOOK WERE DEVELOPED AND TESTED AT JUST OVER 4,000 FEET, SO IF YOU'RE AT A HIGHER OR LOWER ALTITUDE, YOU MAY NEED TO MAKE SOME SMALL ADJUSTMENTS LIKE ADDING A LITTLE MORE FLOUR OR WATER, OR ALLOWING FOR A LONGER RISE TIME.

ENGLISH MUFFIN BREAD

◈ YIELD: 1 LOAF   ◷ PREP: 15M   ⧗ COOK: 30M   ◷ TOTAL TIME: 2 1/5 HRS

If you like English Muffins, then you'll love this recipe! It has a similar flavor and texture to English Muffins but in an easy, no-fuss loaf.

INGREDIENTS

- 3 cups gluten free flour
- 1 tablespoon sugar
- 1 tablespoon instant yeast
- 1 teaspoon salt
- 1/2 cup instant milk powder
- 1/4 teaspoon baking soda
- 2 cups warm water, slightly warmer than room temp
- 2 tablespoons neutral tasting oil such as avocado or vegetable
- cornmeal, to sprinkle in pan

RECIPE NOTES

- While bread is typically best fresh, I prefer this bread sliced and toasted so it tastes more like an English muffin.

ENGLISH MUFFIN BREAD

INSTRUCTIONS

1. Grease a loaf pan with butter and sprinkle with cornmeal. Set aside.
2. Add all ingredients to the bowl of a stand mixer in order listed.
3. Mix on medium speed for 3 minutes. The texture should be between a thick banana bread batter and a regular wheat-based dough (**see page xii**).
4. Turn out onto a floured surface and turn to coat, gently shaping into a loaf.
5. Carefully place the loaf into the prepared pan and cover loosely with plastic wrap.
6. Allow to rise in a warm place for 30-45 minutes or until almost doubled in size.
7. Preheat the oven to 400°F and bake for 25-30 minutes, until the loaf is a light golden brown and the internal temperature is 190°F.
8. Allow bread to cool in the pan for 10 minutes, then transfer to a cooling rack.
9. Cool completely before slicing.
10. This bread tastes great, freshly sliced, and also toasted.
11. The best way to store gluten free bread is to slice, place in a Ziploc freezer bag, remove all the air, seal, and freeze. You can then remove a slice and pop it in the toaster or microwave as you need. It might help to put pieces of wax or parchment paper between the slices so they don't stick together.
12. Once you have frozen the bread, it's best toasted or warmed in the microwave for 10-15 seconds. I don't recommend refrigeration as the bread tends to crumble easily.

BAKING TIP

CONSISTENCY IS KEY! THERE ARE SO MANY THINGS THAT AFFECT THE CONSISTENCY OF BREAD DOUGH SUCH AS HUMIDITY, ALTITUDE, AND THE WAY YOU MEASURE FLOUR. ONCE THE DOUGH HAS BEEN MIXED, COMPARE IT WITH THE PICTURE ON PAGE XII TO SEE IF IT LOOKS SIMILAR. THE TEXTURE SHOULD BE BETWEEN A THICK BANANA BREAD BATTER AND A REGULAR WHEAT-BASED DOUGH: IT SHOULD NOT FORM A BALL AS IT IS MIXED, IT SHOULD BE TOO STICKY TO HANDLE WITH BARE HANDS, BUT DEFINITELY BE CONSIDERED A DOUGH AS OPPOSED TO A BATTER.

FRENCH HERB MINI LOAVES

YIELD: 3 MINI LOAVES PREP: 15M COOK: 25M TOTAL TIME: 1HR

Hearty, easy-to-make mini loaves packed with herbs. This is a delicious bread to serve with soup!

INGREDIENTS

- 2 cups + 2 tablespoons gluten free flour
- 3/4 teaspoon salt
- 1 tablespoon sugar
- 2 teaspoons instant yeast
- 4 teaspoons herbes de Provence
- 1/3 cup instant milk powder
- 1 1/4 cups warm water, slightly warmer than room temp
- 1 tablespoon olive oil

RECIPE NOTES

- Herbes de Provence is a unique seasoning blend that you can find in the spice section of your local grocery store, or online. Be sure to check the label and/or contact the company to ensure that it is a gluten free blend.
- Try serving this bread with a side of soup!
- You can double this recipe and make 6 mini loaves.

THEREISLIFEAFTERWHEAT.COM

FRENCH HERB MINI LOAVES

INSTRUCTIONS

1. Grease 3 mini loaf pans with butter or oil.
2. Add all ingredients to the bowl of a stand mixer in order listed.
3. Mix on medium speed for 2-3 minutes. The texture should be between a thick banana bread batter and a regular wheat-based dough (**see page xii**).
4. Turn out onto a floured surface and turn to coat.
5. Divide dough into 3 equal portions and gently shape each into a loaf.
6. Place each loaf in a prepared pan and cover loosely with plastic wrap. I like to put all 3 pans onto a small baking sheet during proofing and baking as it makes them easier to move.
7. Allow to rise in a warm place for 30-45 minutes, until doubled in size.
8. Preheat the oven to 350°F and bake for 25-30 minutes, until the internal temperature reaches 190°F.
9. Allow the loaves to cool in their pans for 10 minutes before transferring to a cooling rack.
10. Cool completely before slicing.

BAKING TIP

FLOUR MATTERS! GLUTEN FREE FLOURS BEHAVE VERY DIFFERENTLY, ESPECIALLY IN YEAST BREADS AND ROLLS. ALL OF THE RECIPES IN THIS COOKBOOK HAVE BEEN DEVELOPED AND TESTED WITH 2 GLUTEN FREE FLOUR BLENDS THAT I HAVE FOUND TO OUTPERFORM ANY OTHERS WHEN IT COMES TO BAKING GLUTEN FREE BREADS: GFJULES ALL-PURPOSE BLEND, AND MY OWN HOMEMADE RECIPE. YOU CAN FIND A LINK TO GFJULES FLOUR ALONG WITH OTHER BONUS CONTENT AT HTTPS://THEREISLIFEAFTERWHEAT.COM /COOKBOOK, AND THE HOMEMADE FLOUR BLEND RECIPE ON PAGE XV.

FRENCH BREAD

YIELD: 1 LOAF   PREP: 15M   COOK: 35M   TOTAL TIME: 2 1/5 HRS

All the flavor and texture of classic French bread in a delightfully easy, gluten free loaf.

INGREDIENTS

- 3 1/2 cups gluten free flour
- 1 tablespoon instant yeast
- 2 tablespoons sugar
- 1/2 cup instant milk powder
- 1 teaspoon salt
- 2 cups warm water, slightly warmer than room temp
- 2 tablespoons oil

RECIPE NOTES

- Many French bread recipes tell you to toss some water or ice cubes in the bottom of the oven when you put the bread in, but I found that this caused some sogginess on the bottom for gluten free bread so I don't recommend that method.

FRENCH BREAD

INSTRUCTIONS

1. Add all ingredients to the bowl of a stand mixer in order listed.
2. Mix on medium speed for 2-3 minutes. The texture should be between a thick banana bread batter and a regular wheat-based dough (**see page xii**).
3. Turn out onto a floured surface and turn to coat, gently shaping into a loaf about a foot long. Transfer to a parchment-lined baking sheet.
4. Cover loosely with plastic wrap and allow to rise 30-45 minutes in a warm location until close to doubled in size.
5. Preheat oven to 375°F.
6. While the oven is preheating, carefully make 3 slashes across top of bread, 1/2 - 1 inch deep, with a sharp knife.
7. Gently brush with egg wash (you won't use all of it).
8. Bake for 30-40 minutes, until the loaf is golden brown and internal temperature reaches at least 190°F.
9. Allow to cool completely on a wire rack before slicing.

BAKING TIP

LOOKING FOR A
SILVER LINING?
GLUTEN FREE
BREADS ONLY
NEED 1 RISE, SO
THEY'RE EASIER
AND QUICKER TO
MAKE!

SWEET BREADS

BAKING TIP

EGG FREE? BOB'S RED MILL EGG REPLACER WORKS WELL IN MOST OF MY RECIPES! I HAVE TESTED IT WITH RECIPES CONTAINING 1 OR 2 EGGS, BUT THE EGG-RICH RECIPES SUCH AS BRIOCHE MIGHT NOT PERFORM AS WELL.

HONEY BROWN BREAD

YIELD: 3 MINI LOAVES · PREP: 15M · COOK: 25M · TOTAL TIME: 2 HRS

You can find variations of this brown bread served as an appetizer in some restaurants. It is has a slightly sweet, earthy flavor thanks to molasses and a little cocoa powder.

INGREDIENTS

- 2 cups gluten free flour
- ½ tablespoon brown sugar
- 2 teaspoons cocoa powder
- 2 teaspoons instant yeast
- ¾ teaspoon salt
- 2 tablespoons unsalted butter, softened
- 1 cup warm water, slightly warmer than room temp
- 2 tablespoons honey
- 2 tablespoons molasses
- Cornmeal for dusting *optional*

RECIPE NOTES

- You can double this recipe to make 6 mini loaves.
- This bread is best served slightly warm with a schmear of butter.

HONEY BROWN BREAD

INSTRUCTIONS

1. Grease 3 mini loaf pans with butter and sprinkle with cornmeal. Set aside.
2. In a liquid measuring cup or bowl, combine warm water, honey, and molasses until dissolved. Set aside
3. Add all ingredients, including water, honey, and molasses mixture, to the bowl of a stand mixer in order listed.
4. Mix on medium speed for 2-3 minutes. The texture should be between a thick banana bread batter and a regular wheat-based dough (**see page xii**).
5. Turn out onto a floured surface and turn to coat.
6. Divide into 3 equal pieces and gently shape each into a loaf.
7. Carefully place the loaves into the prepared pans and cover loosely with plastic wrap. I set all 3 on a small baking sheet for easy transportation, and keep them there while baking.
8. Allow to rise in a warm place for 30-45 minutes or until almost doubled in size.
9. Preheat the oven to 350°F and bake for 30-35 minutes, until the loaf is a light golden brown and internal temperature is 190°F.
10. Allow bread to cool in the pan for 10 minutes, then transfer to a cooling rack.
11. Cool completely before slicing.
12. The best way to store gluten free bread is to slice, place in a Ziploc freezer bag, remove all the air, seal, and freeze. You can then remove a slice and pop it in the toaster or microwave as you need. It might help to put pieces of wax or parchment paper between the slices so they don't stick together.
13. Once you have frozen the bread, it's best warmed in the microwave for 10-15 seconds. I don't recommend refrigeration as the bread tends to crumble easily.

BAKING TIP

DAIRY FREE?
SUBSTITUTE
COCONUT INSTANT
MILK POWDER AND
USE A BUTTER
SUBSTITUTE IN
STICK FORM.

CINNAMON SWIRL BREAD

◉ YIELD: 1 LOAF ⏱ PREP: 25M ⧖ COOK: 50M ⏱ TOTAL TIME: 2 1/5 HRS

A classic bread swirled with sweet sugar and aromatic cinnamon, just like the kind you would buy in your favorite bakery.

INGREDIENTS

FOR THE BREAD
- 3 cups gluten free flour
- 1 tablespoon instant yeast
- 1 teaspoon salt
- 1/2 cup instant milk powder
- 1/3 cup sugar
- 1 large egg, room temp

- 1 3/4 cup warm water, slightly warmer than room temp
- 1 tablespoon butter, softened

FOR THE FILLING
- 2 tablespoons butter, melted and cooled
- 1/3 cup sugar
- 1 1/2 tablespoons cinnamon

RECIPE NOTES

- It's tempting to dig in while the bread is warm, but it will be best if you wait until fully cooled. It's worth the wait, I promise!
- Try making French toast or bread pudding with the leftovers!

CINNAMON SWIRL BREAD

INSTRUCTIONS

1. Grease bottom and corners of a loaf pan with butter or cooking spray and set aside.
2. Assemble filling by whisking together sugar and cinnamon in a small bowl. Set aside.
3. Add all ingredients to the bowl of a stand mixer in order listed.
4. Mix on medium speed for 3 minutes. The texture should be between a thick banana bread batter and a regular wheat-based dough (**see page xii**).
5. Sprinkle the counter with 1-2 tablespoons of flour and turn dough out onto the surface. Sprinkle another 1-2 tablespoons of flour on top and turn the dough to coat just the outsides.
6. Roll dough out into a rectangle 18 inches long and the width of your bread pan.
7. Brush with melted and cooled butter.
8. Sprinkle with prepared cinnamon sugar
9. Starting at the short end, carefully roll the dough, using a dough scraper as needed if the dough sticks to the counter. Try to make the roll as tight as possible. Seal the end, wetting your fingers if necessary.
10. Gently transfer the loaf to the prepared pan and loosely cover with plastic wrap which has been sprayed with cooking spray.
11. Allow to rise in a warm place for 30-45 minutes, until nearly doubled in size.

INSTRUCTIONS CONTINUED ON NEXT PAGE

CINNAMON SWIRL BREAD

INSTRUCTIONS CONTINUED

12. Preheat the oven to 350°F.
13. Bake for about 50 minutes, until the top is golden brown and a thermometer inserted reads 190°F.
14. Allow bread to cool in the pan for 10 minutes, then transfer to a cooling rack.
15. Cool completely before slicing.
16. Be sure to enjoy it fresh! It is best this way.
17. The best way to store gluten free bread is to slice, place in a Ziploc freezer bag, remove all the air, seal, and freeze. You can then remove a slice and pop it in the toaster or microwave as you need. It might help to put pieces of wax or parchment paper between the slices so they don't stick together.
18. Once you have frozen the bread, it's best toasted or warmed in the microwave for 10-15 seconds. I don't recommend refrigeration as the bread tends to crumble easily.

MALLORCA

YIELD: 12 ROLLS   PREP: 25M   COOK: 20M   TOTAL TIME: 2HRS

Pronounced mai-or-kuh, these Puerto Rican sweet rolls have a distinct, swirled shape, and are slightly sweet. Slice the leftover rolls in half to make Monte Cristo sandwiches or French toast!

INGREDIENTS

FOR THE DOUGH

- 4 1/2 cups gluten free flour
- 1/3 cup white sugar
- 1/2 cup instant milk powder
- 1/2 teaspoon salt
- 1 tablespoon instant yeast
- 2 1/4 cups warm water, slightly warmer than room temp
- 4 large egg yolks, room temp
- 1 stick butter, softened

ADDITIONAL

- 4 tablespoons butter for brushing, melted
- powdered sugar

RECIPE NOTES

- While a shorter rise time will yield beautifully formed rolls like you see in the photo, allowing the mallorca to rise further will give a fluffier, more appealing texture.
- Because this recipe calls for 4 egg yolks, an egg replacement won't likely work.

MALLORCA

INSTRUCTIONS

1. Line a large baking sheet with parchment paper and set aside.
2. Add all dough ingredients to the bowl of a stand mixer in order listed.
3. Mix on medium speed for 3 minutes. The texture should be between a thick banana bread batter and a regular wheat-based dough (**see page xii**).
4. Turn dough out onto a floured surface and roll to coat, being careful not to incorporate extra flour into the dough.
5. Divide dough into 12 equal pieces. Roll the dough pieces into 1/2 inch ropes. Shape the ropes into coiled buns, starting at the center and tucking the end under the bun.
6. Place rolls on a prepared pan, loosely cover with a kitchen towel or plastic wrap and let rise for 30-45 minutes until almost doubled in size.
7. Using a pastry brush, gently brush rolls with about 3 tablespoons of melted butter.
8. Preheat the oven to 350°F and bake for 20-25 minutes, until the rolls are just beginning to brown. Brush with another tablespoon of butter.
9. Allow buns to cool, then sift generously with powdered sugar.
10. Enjoy the buns fresh, they are best this way!
11. Store buns in a sealed plastic bag on the counter for a day or in the freezer.
12. When ready to eat, reheat briefly in the microwave, just until warm.
13. Mallorca makes great Monte Cristo sandwiches and French toast! Just slice to desired thickness and use like you would use bread.

BAKING TIP

IF YOUR BREAD RISES WELL INITIALLY BUT FALLS WHILE BAKING, YOU MIGHT NEED TO ADD A LITTLE EXTRA FLOUR NEXT TIME. CHECK THE PICTURE ON PAGE XIII TO SEE WHAT YOUR DOUGH SHOULD LOOK LIKE.

CINNAMON TWISTS

🌰YIELD: 16-20   🕐PREP: 30M   ⧗COOK: 10M   🕐TOTAL TIME: 2HRS

Made with my popular croissant roll dough from page 72, these cinnamon twists are buttery, flaky, and reminiscent of the leftover pie crust baked with cinnamon sugar your Grandma used to make.

INGREDIENTS

- Croissant dough from page 72.
- 6 tablespoons sugar
- 3 teaspoons cinnamon
- 3 tablespoons butter, melted

CINNAMON TWISTS

INSTRUCTIONS

1. Prepare Croissant dough on pg 72 as directed, through step 8.
2. Prepare cinnamon sugar by whisking together cinnamon and sugar. Set aside.
3. Remove dough from the fridge or freezer and roll out into a rectangle about 1/4 inch thick.
4. Brush the entire rectangle with about half the melted butter.
5. Sprinkle half the dough with about half the cinnamon sugar, then starting with the short end of the dough that isn't covered in cinnamon sugar, carefully lift and fold the dough in half widthwise so you have a sandwich and press down gently.
6. Using a pizza cutter or sharp knife, cut the dough into strips about 1 inch wide by 5 inches long.
7. Gently twist each of the strips 2-3 times.
8. Transfer twists to a baking sheet, leaving about an inch between them.
9. Brush twists with remaining butter, and sprinkle with the rest of the cinnamon sugar.
10. Cover rolls loosely with plastic wrap and allow to rise in a warm location for about 20 minutes until puffy.
11. Bake at 400°F for 8-12 minutes, until golden brown on the bottom.

BAKING TIP

DID YOU KNOW THAT YOU DON'T REALLY NEED TO PROOF YEAST?? IF USING REGULAR YEAST, PROOFING IT FIRST WILL DECREASE THE RISE TIME, BUT WITH INSTANT YEAST THE RISE TIME SHOULD BE ABOUT THE SAME. YAY FOR SIMPLE AND EASY!

CHOCOLATE BABKA

🍞 YIELD: 1 LOAF   🕐 PREP: 30M   ⏳ COOK: 50M   🕐 TOTAL TIME: 3HRS

A sweet braided bread that originated in Jewish communities in Poland and Ukraine. You'll be hard-pressed to find a more beautiful loaf of bread! Babka can be stuffed with a variety of different fillings (cinnamon probably being the most common). The exposed filling and crumb topping create a masterpiece that appears deceptively difficult to make.

INGREDIENTS

FOR THE DOUGH

- 3 cups gluten free flour
- 1/3 cup instant milk powder
- 1 tablespoon instant yeast
- 1 1/4 teaspoon salt
- 1/4 cup sugar
- 1/4 teaspoon cinnamon
- 1/3 cup unsalted butter, room temp
- 1 1/4 cups warm water, slightly warmer than room temp
- 1 large egg, room temp
- 2 teaspoons vanilla extract

FOR THE EGG WASH

- 1 large egg, beaten with a pinch of salt until well-combined (you'll only use about half)

FOR THE FILLING

- 1/4 cup sugar
- 1/4 teaspoon cinnamon
- 3 tablespoons cocoa
- 2 tablespoons butter, melted
- 1/2 cup mini semisweet chocolate chips (see notes)
- 1/2 cup diced pecans or walnuts, toasted *optional*

FOR THE CRUMB TOPPING

- 2 tablespoons butter, melted
- 1/4 teaspoon cinnamon
- 1/3 cup powdered sugar
- 1/4 cup gluten free flour

RECIPE NOTES

- If you can't tolerate pecans or don't like them, feel free to omit them.
- You can use regular-sized chocolate chips, but chop them first so they are in smaller pieces and will be more evenly distributed throughout the loaf.

CHOCOLATE BABKA

INSTRUCTIONS

TO MAKE THE FILLING
- Combine the sugar, cinnamon, and cocoa. Stir in the melted butter.

TO MAKE THE CRUMB TOPPING
- Mix all ingredients together with a fork until crumbly.

TO MAKE THE DOUGH
1. Lightly grease a 9X5 inch loaf pan with butter or cooking spray and set aside.
2. Add all dough ingredients to the bowl of a stand mixer in order listed.
3. Mix on medium speed for 2-3 minutes. The texture should be between a thick banana bread batter and a regular wheat-based dough (**see page xii**).
4. Turn dough out onto a floured surface and roll to coat, being careful not to incorporate extra flour into the dough. Be sure there is enough flour on your work surface so the dough doesn't stick as you roll it out.
5. Roll the dough into a rectangle about 9x18 inches. It should be about ¼ inch thick.
6. Smear the dough with the filling, coming within an inch of the edges.
7. Scatter the nuts and chocolate chips over the top of the filling.
8. Starting with a short end, roll the dough gently and tightly into a log, sealing the seam and ends.

INSTRUCTIONS CONTINUED ON NEXT PAGE

INSTRUCTIONS CONTINUED

9. Use scissors or a sharp knife to cut the log in half lengthwise to make two pieces of dough about 10 inches long. As you cut, try to prevent much filling from spilling out.
10. With the exposed filling side up, twist the two pieces a couple of times into a braid, tucking the ends underneath and pressing gently to seal.
11. Carefully transfer to the prepared pan.
12. Brush with the egg glaze (you'll have quite a bit left over, that's OK) and sprinkle with the topping, pressing gently so it will stick.
13. Cover loosely with plastic wrap that has been sprayed with cooking spray and allow to rise in a warm location until about doubled in size.
14. Preheat the oven to 300°F and bake for 50-55 minutes until it's a deep golden brown and the internal temperature has reached at least 190°F.
15. Remove from the oven and immediately loosen the edges with a heatproof spatula or table knife.
16. Allow to cool for 10 minutes, then turn out onto a rack to cool completely.
17. Slice and serve at room temperature, or warm briefly in the microwave or toaster.

APPLE PULL APART BREAD

⊛ YIELD: 1 LOAF   ⏱ PREP: 30M   ⏲ COOK: 40M   ⏰ TOTAL TIME: 2HRS

All the flavor of an apple fritter in a beautiful pull-apart loaf!

INGREDIENTS

FOR THE DOUGH

- 3 cups gluten free flour (gfJules)
- 1 teaspoon salt
- 1 tablespoon instant yeast
- 1/2 cup instant milk powder
- 1 1/2 cup warm water, slightly warmer than room temp
- 1 large egg, room temp
- 2 tablespoons butter
- 1/2 cup sweetened condensed milk

FOR THE FILLING

- 2 medium Granny Smith apples, peeled, cored, thinly sliced and chopped into 1/2 inch pieces
- 2 tablespoons butter, melted
- 1/2 cup packed brown sugar
- 2 teaspoons ground cinnamon

FOR THE GLAZE

- 1 cup powdered sugar
- 3-5 teaspoons half and half or water

RECIPE NOTES

- Although granny smith are my favorite, you can use any other apple that works well in baked goods such as fuji or gala.
- You can use sweetened condensed coconut milk, powdered coconut milk, and a dairy free butter substitute in stick form in this recipe if you need to make it dairy free.

APPLE PULL APART BREAD

INSTRUCTIONS

1. Grease bottom and corners of a loaf pan with butter or cooking spray and set aside.
2. Assemble filling by stirring all ingredients together in a bowl. Set aside.
3. Add all ingredients to bowl of stand mixer in order listed.
4. Mix on medium speed for 3 minutes. The texture should be between a thick banana bread batter and a regular wheat-based dough (**see page xii**).
5. Sprinkle counter with 1-2 tablespoons of flour and turn dough out onto surface. Sprinkle another 1-2 tablespoons of flour on top and turn the dough to coat just the outsides.
6. Roll dough out into a rectangle about 14X10 inches.
7. Top evenly with apple mixture.
8. Using a pizza cutter, cut into a 4X4 grid making 16 squares (they won't be perfect squares, that's OK)
9. Stand loaf pan up vertically (so that the short end is on the counter) and carefully stack the squares in the loaf pan.
10. Cover loosely with a piece of plastic wrap that has been sprayed with cooking spray and rise 30-45 minutes in a warm location until nearly doubled in size.
11. Bake at 350°F about 40 minutes, until bread is golden brown on top and done in the middle.
12. Allow to cool at least half an hour.
13. While bread is cooling, make the glaze by whisking together powdered sugar and milk of choice, then drizzle over the loaf of bread and serve immediately.
14. Be sure to enjoy it fresh! It is best this way.
15. Store, covered, in the fridge for up to 3 days or freeze the leftovers. When ready to eat, warm briefly in the microwave.

BAKING TIP

NOT ALL
YEASTS ARE
GLUTEN FREE,
SO BE SURE
TO CHECK
LABELS!

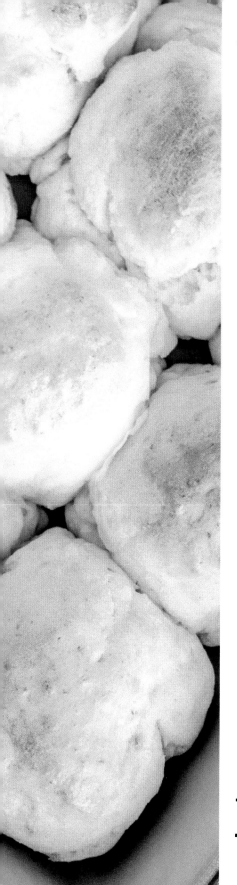

ROLLS

BAKING TIP

WATCHING YOUR
SODIUM INTAKE?
FEEL FREE TO
REDUCE THE SALT
IN ANY RECIPE.
FOR BEST RESULTS,
DO NOT REDUCE
MORE THAN 50%.

DINNER ROLLS

👤 YIELD: 12 ROLLS   🕐 PREP: 15M   ⏳ COOK: 15M   🕐 TOTAL TIME: 1HR

These gluten free rolls are perfectly soft, fluffy, and so easy to make! They are the perfect addition to any meal and will be enjoyed by everyone, gluten-eaters included.

INGREDIENTS

- 3 cups gluten free flour
- 1 tablespoon instant yeast
- 3 tablespoons sugar
- 1 teaspoon salt
- 1/3 cup instant milk powder
- 1/4 cup butter, softened
- 1 large egg, room temp
- 1 1/2 cups warm water, slightly warmer than room temp

RECIPE NOTES

- These rolls make great sandwiches! We often serve them for Thanksgiving dinner and use them for turkey sandwiches over the next few days.
- Keep a small bowl of oil by you while you shape the rolls, to keep your hands from getting sticky.

DINNER ROLLS

INSTRUCTIONS

1. Grease a 9X13 inch pan with butter and set aside.
2. Add all ingredients to the bowl of a stand mixer in order listed.
3. Mix on medium speed for 3 minutes. The texture should be between a thick banana bread batter and a regular wheat-based dough (**see page xii**).
4. Because the dough is sticky, you'll want to coat your hands in oil so you can easily handle it. Divide the dough into 12 equal pieces and form into balls with oiled hands. You might need to re-apply oil a few times.
5. Place the balls of dough in a 9X13 inch baking pan and cover the pan with plastic wrap or a light towel.
6. Allow to rise in a warm location for 30-45 minutes until nearly doubled in size.
7. Preheat the oven to 350°F and bake for 17-20 minutes, until golden brown on top and done inside. If you omit the instant milk powder, the rolls might not brown as much so check the inside if they aren't browned by 20 minutes.
8. Remove from the oven and brush with melted butter. These rolls are best served warm but we put the leftovers in a Ziploc bag and they were still soft the next day.
9. This recipe freezes well.

BAKING TIP

DID YOU KNOW THAT I HAVE A FULL PAGE OF BONUS CONTENT AVAILABLE EXCLUSIVELY FOR OWNERS OF THIS COOKBOOK? FIND STEP-BY-STEP VIDEOS, LINKS TO MY FAVORITE PRODUCTS, AND MORE AT HTTPS://THEREISLIFEAFTERWHEAT.COM/COOKBOOK

CLOVERLEAF ROLLS

YIELD: 9 ROLLS **PREP: 20M** **COOK: 15M** **TOTAL TIME: 1HR**

These gluten free cloverleaf rolls are soft, fluffy, and packed with flavor! As if that wasn't enough, they're also easy to make and ready in about an hour - the perfect complement to any meal.

INGREDIENTS

- 2 cups gluten free flour
- 1 tablespoon instant yeast
- 2 tablespoons sugar
- 1/4 teaspoon baking powder
- 3/4 teaspoon salt
- 1 large egg, room temp
- 1/2 cup + 2 tablespoons warm water, slightly warmer than room temp
- 1/2 cup oil

- 1 teaspoon Italian seasoning
- 1/3 cup freshly grated parmesan cheese

FOR THE GARLIC BUTTER

- 1 tablespoon unsalted butter
- 1/8 teaspoon (or more to taste) garlic salt

RECIPE NOTES

- While either of my 2 recommended gluten free flour blends will work well with this recipe, Namaste brand is also a great fit here and provides a more robust flavor profile.

CLOVERLEAF ROLLS

INSTRUCTIONS

1. Grease 9 wells of a muffin tin with cooking spray or oil. Set aside.
2. In the bowl of a stand mixer, add flour, yeast, sugar, baking powder, salt, egg, water, and oil.
3. Mix on medium speed for 2 minutes. The texture should be between a thick banana bread batter and a regular wheat-based dough (**see page xii**).
4. Add Italian seasoning and parmesan cheese, and mix until combined.
5. In a small bowl, melt 1 tablespoon of butter. Stir in garlic salt.
6. Rub a small amount of the garlic butter onto your hands, pinch off about a 1 tablespoon size piece and roll it into a ball between your hands.
7. Place 3 of these balls side-by-side in each well of the muffin tin. They should be pretty cozy and fill a large portion of the well.
8. Repeat with the remainder of dough.
9. Cover the rolls loosely with plastic wrap and allow to rise in a warm place for 20-40 minutes, until they are almost doubled in size.
10. Preheat oven to 350°F.
11. Remove plastic wrap and bake for about 15 minutes, until rolls are a light golden brown and done inside.
12. Allow to cool for 30 minutes before serving.

BAKING TIP

HAVE A QUESTION ABOUT ONE OF THESE RECIPES? FILL OUT THE CONTACT FORM AT

HTTPS://THEREISLIFEAFTERWHEAT.COM /COOKBOOK

AND I'LL GET BACK TO YOU SOON.

BRIOCHE ROLLS

YIELD: 12 ROLLS   PREP: 20M   COOK: 15M   TOTAL TIME: 1 1/2HRS

These gluten free brioche rolls are a re-creation of a traditional French sweet bread. Brioche has a unique flavor and texture, a sort of melt-in-your-mouth experience. It is delightful fresh out of the oven, as part of a sandwich, or any way you might enjoy bread.

INGREDIENTS

- 2 3/4 cups gluten free flour
- 2 teaspoons instant yeast
- 1 teaspoon salt
- 1/4 cup sugar
- 3 large eggs, room temp
- 1/3 cup milk
- 1/2 cup unsalted butter, room temp
- 1 teaspoon vinegar

RECIPE NOTES

- Because of the amount of eggs called for in this recipe, an egg substitute might not work as well.
- My family's favorite way to enjoy brioche rolls is with a side of raspberry jam.

BRIOCHE ROLLS

INSTRUCTIONS

1. Thoroughly grease 12 brioche molds or a muffin tin that makes 12 muffins. Set aside.
2. In the bowl of a stand mixer, measure gluten free flour. Add yeast, sugar, salt, eggs, milk, and vinegar and mix on low speed until smooth.
3. Add butter 1 tablespoon at a time, mixing for 20 seconds between each addition. The texture should be between a thick banana bread batter and a regular wheat-based dough (**see page xii**).
4. **If making in a muffin tin**, divide dough evenly to make 12 rolls and smooth the tops with a spatula.
5. **If making in brioche molds**, sprinkle 2-3 tablespoons of gluten free flour onto the counter and coat the dough in the flour so it's workable. Don't mix the flour into the dough, and only use as much as you need. The more flour you use, the more dense your dough will be and the harder it will be for it to rise.
6. Divide dough into 12 equal pieces. Reserve a small section of each piece to make the traditional topknot, it will be a ball about 1/2 inch in diameter.
7. Place each of the 12 larger pieces into brioche molds, and smooth tops. Make a small indent in the center of each and place the 1/2 inch ball in the indentation of each roll.
8. Cover loosely with greased plastic wrap and let rise in a warm, draft-free area for 30-45 minutes until about doubled in size.
9. Bake at 350°F for 15-20 minutes until they are done. Traditional brioche will be a dark brown color, but gluten free flours don't produce that kind of color, so don't wait until they're brown :)
10. These rolls are best served fresh, but can be frozen and warmed in the microwave.

BAKING TIP

DID YOU KNOW THAT GLUTEN FREE DOUGHS DO NOT REQUIRE KNEADING? THAT'S BECAUSE THE PROCESS OF KNEADING IS USED TO DEVELOP GLUTEN, AND WE DON'T HAVE TO WORRY ABOUT THAT! SO GO AHEAD, SAVE YOURSELF SOME TIME AND EFFORT BY SKIPPING THAT STEP.

CRESCENT ROLLS

🌲YIELD: 8 ROLLS   🕐PREP: 20M   ⏳COOK: 15M   🕐TOTAL TIME: 1HR 20M

Soft, tender, and light gluten free crescent rolls are SO EASY to make! They will be ready in about 1 hour, and they are the perfect addition to any meal.

INGREDIENTS

- 2 cups gluten free flour
- 1 tablespoon instant yeast
- 3 tablespoons sugar or honey
- 1/4 teaspoon baking powder
- 1/2 teaspoon salt (increase to 1 teaspoon if using oil or unsalted butter)
- 1/2 cup + 2 tablespoons warm water, slightly warmer than room temp
- 1 large egg, room temp
- 1/2 cup butter, almost melted OR neutral oil
- Extra butter to brush when done

RECIPE NOTES

- You can use this dough in any recipe calling for canned crescent roll dough.
- It is great as a pizza crust or for pizza rolls or chicken pillows.

CRESCENT ROLLS

INSTRUCTIONS

1. In bowl of stand mixer, measure gluten free flour, yeast, sugar or honey, baking powder, and salt.
2. Add warm water, egg, and 1/2 cup butter or oil, and mix with paddle attachment on medium speed for 3 minutes. The texture should be between a thick banana bread batter and a regular wheat-based dough (**see page xii**)
3. Lightly dust countertop or a pie crust bag with gluten free flour.
4. Scrape the dough into a ball shape on your dusted area and sprinkle a little more starch over the top of your dough to prevent it from sticking. If using a pie crust bag, remove air and zip it up.
5. Using a rolling pin, roll dough out to a 12-inch circle. Using a pizza slicer (or very sharp knife) that has been dusted in flour, cut the circle into 8 wedges like you would slice a pizza.
6. Carefully roll each wedge inward to form a crescent. If dough sticks to the counter, gently pinch the end to secure the roll so it won't lose shape as it bakes.
7. Gently place a few inches apart on a baking sheet and curve them slightly to form a crescent shape.

INSTRUCTIONS CONTINUED ON NEXT PAGE

CRESCENT ROLLS

INSTRUCTIONS CONTINUED

9. Let rolls rise in a warm location for 20-40 minutes until they are close to doubled in size.
10. Bake for 9-12 minutes at 350°F. Gluten free breads tend to not brown as much, so don't wait for these to be well browned before pulling them out or they may dry out. Flake with a fork in the center of a roll to see if it's done. Mine were done in about 11 minutes.
11. Brush with melted butter or oil and serve warm for best results. Store leftovers in an airtight container or bread bag at room temp for a day or two, or in the freezer. These can easily be re-warmed by wrapping in foil and placing in a 325°F oven for about 5 minutes from fridge or 10 minutes from freezer.

CROISSANTS

YIELD: 8   PREP: 45M   COOK: 20M   TOTAL TIME: 4HRS

Buttery, flaky, and tender, these rolls are worth the extra time and effort! You can use the prepared dough any way you might use the pop-able cans of crescent rolls found in the grocery store.

INGREDIENTS

DOUGH

- 2 1/4 cups gluten free flour
- 2 teaspoons instant yeast
- 2 tablespoons sugar
- 1 teaspoon salt
- 1 cup warm water, slightly warmer than room temp
- 2 tablespoons unsalted butter

LAMINATING

- 3/4 cup unsalted butter

EGG WASH

- 1 large egg, beaten
- 1 teaspoon water, milk, or cream

RECIPE NOTES

- When rolling out the dough during the lamination process, keep some extra gluten free flour close by to sprinkle on your work surface or rolling pin so the dough doesn't stick.
- You'll be rolling the dough very thin, and it's OK if the sizes don't perfectly match up. Just do the best you can!
- Don't skimp on refrigeration time, it is crucial to forming those beautiful flaky layers, and also helps the butter stay in the roll instead of leaking out while baking.
- Do not refrigerate the dough for more than 24 hours, or the yeast will start to ferment and you'll end up with a sourdough-like flavor.

CROISSANTS

INSTRUCTIONS

1. Add all dough ingredients to the bowl of a stand mixer in order listed.
2. Mix on medium speed for 2-3 minutes. The texture should be between a thick banana bread batter and a regular wheat-based dough (**see page xii**).
3. Turn dough out onto a floured surface and roll to coat, being careful not to incorporate extra flour into the dough. Make sure there is enough flour on the counter to prevent the dough from sticking as you roll it.
4. Divide dough into 12 equal pieces.
5. Take one piece of dough and use a rolling pin to roll it out into a rectangle approximately 5X9 inches. Use more flour as needed, it will be quite thin.
6. Gently spread about 1 tablespoon of butter evenly all over the dough.
7. Take another piece of dough and roll it into the same size and stack it on top of the first piece. Apply a generous amount of butter and spread evenly all over. Repeat to produce a multi-layered dough with alternating layers of rolled out rectangular-shaped dough and butter, ending with a layer of dough.
8. Wrap the stacked dough with plastic wrap and refrigerate for at least an hour or overnight to cool down completely.

INSTRUCTIONS CONTINUED ON NEXT PAGE

CROISSANTS

INSTRUCTIONS CONTINUED

9. Take out the stacked dough and roll it out into a larger rectangle, approximately 10X18 inches.
10. Make 3 even horizontal cuts using a pizza cutter to form 4 smaller rectangles, and cut each of these rectangles in half diagonally to form 8 triangles (or initially cut dough in a zigzag pattern into 8 equal triangles).
11. Take each triangle and tightly roll it up from the base of the triangle into a crescent shape. Tuck the tip underneath and place the croissant with the tip side down onto a parchment-lined baking pan. This is important because if the tip is not tucked under, it will rise and possibly detach from the croissant. Repeat with the rest of the triangles, and place them 2-inches apart on the baking pan.
12. Let the croissants rise in a warm location for 20-30 minutes, until almost doubled in size.
13. Gently brush each croissant with egg wash.
14. Bake at 425°F for 10 minutes. With croissants still in the oven, reduce heat to 375°F and bake another 10-15 minutes until croissants are golden brown.
15. Allow to cool on a wire rack for at least 10 minutes.

JAPANESE MILK BREAD ROLLS

⊛ YIELD: 8 ROLLS　🕐 PREP: 20M　⧗ COOK: 30M　🕐 TOTAL TIME: 2HRS

Japanese Milk Rolls have a soft, chewy structure with a sweet, rich flavor thanks to the unique process involving a starter cooked on the stove.

INGREDIENTS

FOR THE TANGZHONG (STARTER)
- 3 tablespoons water
- 3 tablespoons whole milk
- 2 tablespoons gluten free flour

FOR THE DOUGH
- 2 1/2 cups gluten free flour
- 2 tablespoons instant milk powder

- 1/4 cup sugar
- 1 teaspoon salt
- 1 tablespoon instant yeast
- 1 cup + 2 tablespoons whole milk
- 1 large egg, room temp
- 4 tablespoons unsalted butter, melted

RECIPE NOTES

- Serve these rolls any way you would serve dinner rolls.

JAPANESE MILK BREAD ROLLS

INSTRUCTIONS

To make the tangzhong:

1. Combine all of the ingredients in a small saucepan, and whisk until no lumps remain.
2. Cook the mixture over low heat, whisking constantly, until it is thick and the whisk leaves lines on the bottom of the pan. This should take about 3 minutes.
3. Let it cool to room temperature.

To make the dough:

1. Combine the tangzhong with the remaining dough ingredients in the bowl of a stand mixer and mix for 3 minutes on medium speed. The texture should be between a thick banana bread batter and a regular wheat-based dough (**see page xii**).
2. Turn the dough out onto a lightly floured surface, divide into 8 equal pieces, and shape each piece into a ball.
3. Place the rolls in a greased 9-inch round cake pan.
4. Cover loosely with plastic wrap that has been sprayed with cooking spray and allow to rise in a warm place for 30-45 minutes, until almost doubled in size.
5. Preheat the oven to 350°F.
6. Gently brush the rolls with milk or an egg that has been beaten well.
7. Bake for 25-30 minutes, until the rolls are lightly browned on top and internal temperature reaches 190°F.
8. Allow rolls to cool in the pan for at least 15 minutes before serving.

BAKING TIP

WHAT IS GLUTEN? GLUTEN IS THE BINDING AGENT IN REGULAR FLOUR THAT HOLDS YOUR BAKED GOODS TOGETHER. GLUTEN FREE FLOURS DO NOT, OBVIOUSLY, CONTAIN GLUTEN SO THEY ARE PRONE TO BEING CRUMBLY AND DRY IF YOU DON'T ADD SOME SORT OF BINDING AGENT SUCH AS XANTHAN GUM. BOTH OF THE FLOUR BLENDS I RECOMMEND CONTAIN XANTHAN GUM AND PRODUCE LIGHT, FLUFFY RESULTS!

SWEET ROLLS

BAKING TIP

ALL YEAST BREADS AND ROLLS
REQUIRE RISE TIME IN ORDER TO
ACHIEVE A LIGHT AND FLUFFY
TEXTURE. WHILE SIMPLY ALLOWING
THE DOUGH TO RISE AT ROOM
TEMPERATURE WILL WORK, IT WILL
TAKE MUCH LONGER; HERE ARE
SOME MORE EFFECTIVE RISING
METHODS:

1. USE PROOF SETTING ON OVEN.
2. PREHEAT OVEN TO 100°F, THEN
   TURN OFF AND PLACE DOUGH
   INSIDE WITH THE DOOR CLOSED.
3. PREHEAT OVEN AND LET THE
   DOUGH RISE ON TOP OF THE
   WARM OVEN.

CINNAMON ROLLS

⊕ YIELD: 8 ROLLS   ⊙ PREP: 25M   ⧗ COOK: 25M   ⊙ TOTAL TIME: 1-2HRS

A classic! These cinnamon rolls are light, fluffy, and every bit as good as the gluten-filled ones you remember.

INGREDIENTS

FOR THE DOUGH
- 2 cups flour
- 1 tablespoon instant yeast
- 1/3 cup instant milk powder
- 1/4 cup sugar
- 1 large egg, room temp
- 1/3 cup neutral oil such as avocado or canola oil
- 3/4 teaspoon salt
- 2/3 cup warm water, slightly warmer than room temp

FILLING
- 1/4 cup butter, softened
- 1/4 cup white sugar
- 1/4 cup brown sugar
- 1 1/2 tablespoons cinnamon

CREAM CHEESE FROSTING
- 3 oz cream cheese, softened
- 1/4 cup butter, softened
- 1 cup powdered sugar
- 1/2 teaspoon vanilla extract
- dash salt

RECIPE NOTES

- Try experimenting with different fillings! You can use lemon curd, raspberry jam or pie filling, or try adding about ¼ cup mini chocolate chips with the cinnamon sugar.
- Be sure you have enough flour sprinkled on your surface before rolling.
- Use a dough scraper when rolling the dough if it starts sticking to your surface.

CINNAMON ROLLS

INSTRUCTIONS

1. Lightly grease an 8 or 9-inch cake pan with butter or cooking spray and set aside.
2. Prepare cinnamon sugar by whisking together white sugar, brown sugar, and cinnamon.
3. Add all dough ingredients to the bowl of a stand mixer in order listed.
4. Mix on medium speed for 2-3 minutes. The texture should be between a thick banana bread batter and a regular wheat-based dough (**see page xii**).
5. Turn dough out onto a floured surface and roll to coat, being careful not to incorporate extra flour into the dough. Make sure there is enough flour on the counter to prevent the dough from sticking as you roll it.
6. Roll the dough out in a rectangle about 16X11 inches. If the rolling pin sticks to the dough, sprinkle a little more flour on.
7. Gently spread the softened butter over the dough, then sprinkle it with cinnamon sugar.
8. Starting at the longer end, roll the dough tightly and press to seal.
9. Slice into 8 equal pieces and transfer them to the prepared pan.
10. Cover loosely with plastic wrap and allow to rise in a warm location for about 45 minutes, until doubled in size.
11. Bake at 350°F for 20-25 minutes, until beginning to brown on top and done inside.
12. Make the frosting by mixing cream cheese and butter until smooth and creamy. Add powdered sugar, vanilla, and salt and mix just until smooth. Spread over cinnamon rolls and serve.
13. Store leftovers in a sealed container at room temperature for a day or two, or keep in the freezer. Before serving, briefly reheat in the microwave to soften the cinnamon roll.

BAKING TIP

DOES YOUR LOAF HAVE A SOGGY BOTTOM LAYER? THIS MIGHT BE BECAUSE YOU ALLOWED THE BREAD TO COOL TOO LONG IN THE PAN. ALLOW FOR 10 MINUTES AFTER REMOVING FROM THE OVEN, THEN TRANSFER TO A COOLING RACK.

KOLACHES

⊛ YIELD: 25 PIECES   ⊙ PREP: 25M   ⊗ COOK: 15M   ⊙ TOTAL TIME: 2HRS

A sweet pastry with a fruity filling originating in Czechoslovakia, kolaches are a beautiful pastry perfect for serving at parties or enjoying at home. Traditionally filled with fruit, you can also use a cheese filling (my personal favorite, see notes), or even savory fillings, though you will only find those in the USA. The sour cream enriched dough is delicious and also easy to work with.

INGREDIENTS

DOUGH
- 1 cup sour cream, room temp
- 1/2 cup sugar
- 1/2 cup unsalted butter, melted
- 2 teaspoons salt
- 3/4 cup warm water, slightly warmer than room temp
- 4 cups gluten free flour
- 1 tablespoon instant yeast
- 2 large eggs, room temp

EGG WASH
- 1 large egg, room temp
- 1 teaspoon water, milk, or cream

CHEESE FILLING
- 8 oz cream cheese, softened
- 1/3 cup sugar
- 1 large egg yolk, room temp
- 1/2 teaspoon vanilla extract
- 1/8 teaspoon almond extract

POSIPKA TOPPING
- 1/4 cup gluten free flour
- 1/3 cup sugar
- 2 tablespoons butter, melted

KOLACHES

RECIPE NOTES

- My favorite filling is the cheese filling, they taste just like a cheese Danish!
- The filling will expand a little as the kolaches bake, so don't over-fill.
- You can use 1 filling recipe for the entire batch, or a variety of fillings. Keep in mind that if you use a variety, you won't need the full amount listed in the recipe above.
- When shaping the dough into balls, keep some extra flour close by to use as needed to prevent it from sticking to your hands. Form both hands in a cupping shape around the dough, and gently turn clockwise, pressing as needed, to form a smooth ball.

OTHER FILLING IDEAS

- Prepared pie filling
- Lemon curd
- Preserves - be sure to use good quality, thick preserves

INSTRUCTIONS

CHEESE FILLING
1. Mix cream cheese and sugar on medium speed for 2-3 minutes until soft and creamy.
2. Add egg yolk, vanilla, and almond extract and mix until combined.

KOLACHES

INSTRUCTIONS CONTINUED

1. Prepare fillings and set aside.
2. In a small saucepan, melt butter. Stir in sour cream, sugar, salt, and warm water until smooth.
3. In the bowl of a stand mixer, add gluten free flour, yeast, eggs, and sour cream mixture and mix on medium speed for 2-3 minutes. The texture should be between a thick banana bread batter and a regular wheat-based dough (**see page xii**).
4. Turn out onto a lightly floured surface and divide into about 25 equal pieces.
5. Using a little additional flour as needed, gently roll into balls and transfer them to prepared baking sheets.
6. Gently flatten the balls to between 1/4 and 1/2 inch thick.
7. Using your fingers or a tablespoon, make a wide and deep indent in each piece of dough. Keep in mind the indentation will decrease a little as it bakes, so think deep but be sure there is still a little dough underneath.
8. Scoop about 2 teaspoons of filling into each indentation.
9. Gently brush the dough with egg wash, being careful not to brush the filling.
10. Sprinkle with posipka topping if you want.
11. Cover loosely with plastic wrap and allow to rise in a warm location for 45 minutes to an hour, until kolaches are almost doubled in size.
12. Preheat the oven to 375°F.
13. Bake for 12-15 minutes until they're golden brown.
14. Remove from the oven and allow to cool a little before serving.
15. Enjoy them fresh, they're best this way!
16. Store any leftovers in an airtight container or Ziploc for a few days, or in the freezer for longer. If they get dry or crumbly, warm them briefly in the microwave.

MONKEY BREAD

👤 YIELD: 1 BUNDT PAN　🕐 PREP: 30M　⏱ COOK: 30M　🕐 TOTAL TIME: 2HRS

Fluffy pillows of dough coated in delightful cinnamon sugar and drizzled with vanilla glaze, it's just like what you remember your mom or grandma making!

INGREDIENTS

FOR THE DOUGH

- 4 cups gluten free flour
- 2 tablespoons instant yeast
- 2/3 cup instant milk powder
- 1/3 cup sugar
- 2 large eggs, room temp
- 2/3 cup neutral oil such as avocado or canola oil
- 1 1/2 teaspoons salt
- 1 1/3 cups warm water, slightly warmer than room temp

FOR THE CINNAMON SUGAR

- 1 cup brown sugar
- 4 teaspoons cinnamon
- 1/2 cup butter, melted

FOR THE GLAZE

- 1 cup powdered sugar
- 2 tablespoons heavy cream
- 1 teaspoon vanilla extract

RECIPE NOTES

- Monkey bread is best served warm!
- Invert the monkey bread just after removing from the oven to ensure all the cinnamon sugar goodness stays with the bread instead of sticking to the pan.
- If you have leftovers, warm them briefly in the microwave before serving.

MONKEY BREAD

INSTRUCTIONS

FOR THE CINNAMON SUGAR

1. Whisk together brown sugar and cinnamon. Set aside.

FOR THE DOUGH

1. Add all dough ingredients to the bowl of a stand mixer in order listed.
2. Mix on medium speed for 2-3 minutes. The texture should be between a thick banana bread batter and a regular wheat-based dough (**see page xii**).
3. Turn dough out onto a floured surface and roll to coat, being careful not to incorporate extra flour into the dough.
4. Divide dough into about 30 equal pieces
5. Roll each piece first in butter and then in cinnamon sugar and layer pieces in a well-greased bundt pan.
6. Pour remaining butter and sugar over the top of the rolls.
7. Cover with sprayed plastic wrap and allow to rise for 30-45 minutes in a warm location.
8. Bake at 350ºF for 30 minutes.
9. While baking combine icing ingredients.
10. While still warm, invert the bundt pan to serve and drizzle icing over the top of the Monkey Bread.

BAKING TIP

WHEN MIXING
GLUTEN FREE
BREAD DOUGH,
ALWAYS USE THE
PADDLE
ATTACHMENT.

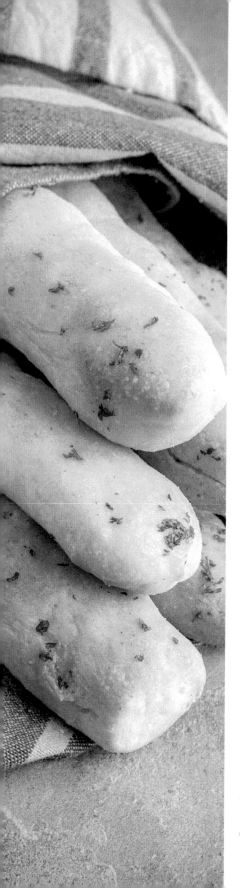

BREADSTICKS AND BUNS

BAKING TIP

TO STORE GLUTEN FREE
BAKED GOODS, ALLOW TO
COOL COMPLETELY THEN
PLACE IN A FREEZER BAG,
PRESS OUT ALL THE AIR,
SEAL, AND STORE IN THE
FREEZER. YOU MIGHT
WANT TO SLICE BEFORE
YOU FREEZE SO IT IS EASY
TO PULL OUT AS MUCH AS
YOU NEED.

GARLIC KNOTS

YIELD: 16 PIECES   PREP: 30M   COOK: 15M   TOTAL TIME: 1 1/2HRS

These buttery garlic knots are packed with flavor and have the perfect texture! When I baked these to take the photos for this cookbook, my kids had friends over and the garlic knots disappeared in minutes - everyone loved them!

INGREDIENTS

DOUGH

- 2 cups gluten free flour
- 1 tablespoon instant yeast
- 1/3 cup instant milk powder
- 2 tablespoons sugar
- 1 large egg, room temp
- 1/3 cup olive oil
- 1/2 teaspoon salt
- 2/3 cup warm water, slightly warmer than room temp

TOPPING

- 1/3 cup unsalted butter, melted
- 3/4 teaspoon garlic salt
- 1 teaspoon Italian seasoning
- optional after baking: 1/4 cup grated Parmesan cheese
- optional after baking: 2 tablespoons chopped fresh parsley

RECIPE NOTES

- Be sure to bake until the rolls are a light golden brown on top, it makes the garlic knots a little crisp on the outside but nice and chewy in the middle.

GARLIC KNOTS

INSTRUCTIONS

1. Line 2 large baking sheets with parchment. Set aside.
2. Add all dough ingredients to the bowl of a stand mixer in order listed.
3. Mix on medium speed for 2-3 minutes. The texture should be between a thick banana bread batter and a regular wheat-based dough (**see page xii**).
4. Turn dough out onto a floured surface and roll to coat, being careful not to incorporate extra flour into the dough.
5. Divide dough into 2 equal pieces and roll each into a rope 20 inches long.
6. Cut each rope into 8 equal pieces.
7. Gently tie each piece of dough rope into a knot and carefully transfer to the prepared baking sheets.
8. Cover loosely with plastic wrap that has been sprayed with cooking spray.
9. Allow to rise in a warm location for 30-45 minutes, until rolls have puffed up to almost doubled in size.
10. Preheat the oven to 400°F.
11. While the oven is preheating, combine butter, garlic salt, and Italian seasoning and gently brush over rolls.
12. Bake for about 15 minutes, until rolls are lightly browned and done inside.
13. If you want, sprinkle rolls with parmesan cheese and fresh parsley before serving.

BAKING TIP

IF BREADS OR ROLLS
HAVE BECOME
CRUMBLY, OR THEY
ARE STORED IN THE
FREEZER, SIMPLY
REHEAT BY BRIEFLY
WARMING IN THE
MICROWAVE, OR
POPPING BREAD IN
THE TOASTER.

CHEESY BREADSTICKS

(†)YIELD: 16 BREADSTICKS (○)PREP: 20M (⊗)COOK: 10M (○)TOTAL TIME: 1HR

This recipe is reminiscent of the fluffy, crispy-on-the-outside and chewy-in-the-middle cheesy breads you can get at your favorite pizza place. They're also super easy to make and ready in an hour!

INGREDIENTS

DOUGH

- 2 cups gluten free flour
- 1 tablespoon instant yeast
- 1/3 cup instant milk powder
- 2 tablespoons sugar
- 1 large egg, room temp
- 1/3 cup olive oil
- 1/2 teaspoon garlic salt
- 2/3 cup warm water, slightly warmer than room temp

TOPPING

- 1 1/2 tablespoons salted butter, melted
- 2 cloves garlic, minced
- 1/3 cup freshly grated parmesan cheese
- 1 1/4 cups shredded mozzarella cheese or pizza cheese blend

RECIPE NOTES

- Try using the dough as a pizza crust! Just follow the same preparation steps, allowing the crust to rise before putting on the toppings.
- You can use any type of cheese or combination of cheeses for the topping. My favorite is a simple packaged, pre-shredded pizza blend.
- If you're feeding a crowd, feel free to double the recipe, separating the dough into 2 sections and baking on two separate baking sheets or pizza stones.

CHEESY BREADSTICKS

INSTRUCTIONS

1. Add all dough ingredients to the bowl of a stand mixer in order listed.
2. Mix on medium speed for 2-3 minutes. The texture should be between a thick banana bread batter and a regular wheat-based dough (**see page xii**).
3. Place a piece of parchment paper (about the size of a large baking sheet) on your counter and sprinkle a tablespoon or two of flour on it.
4. Turn dough out onto the floured parchment paper and roll to coat, being careful not to incorporate extra flour into the dough.
5. Roll out into an oval or rectangle about 1/3 inch thick.
6. Carefully transfer to an upside down baking sheet and cover loosely with plastic wrap.
7. Allow to rise in a warm location for about 30 minutes, until breadsticks have puffed up to almost doubled in size.
8. Preheat the oven to 475°F with a pizza stone or upside down baking sheet on the middle rack.
9. While the oven is preheating, combine butter, and garlic and gently brush over breadsticks.
10. Sprinkle evenly with parmesan and mozzarella cheese.
11. Carefully transfer the breadsticks to the hot pizza stone or upside down baking sheet and bake for 8-12 minutes until golden and bubbly.

BAKING TIP

WHEN MIXING DOUGH, REFERENCE PAGE XII TO BE SURE YOU HAVE THE RIGHT CONSISTENCY. IF YOU THINK YOUR DOUGH IS TOO WET AND STICKY, TRY ADDING A TABLESPOON OR TWO OF FLOUR. IF IT SEEMS TOO THICK, ADD A TABLESPOON OR TWO OF WATER.

BREADSTICKS

⊕ YIELD: 10 ⏱ PREP: 25M ⧗ COOK: 15M ⊙ TOTAL TIME: 1HR

You know those buttery, salty breadsticks you used to enjoy at your favorite Italian restaurant? Yeah, we missed those too! That's why I created this recipe, which is every bit as good as the ones you remember and soooo easy to make in your own kitchen.

INGREDIENTS

DOUGH
- 4 cups gluten free flour
- 2 tablespoons instant yeast
- 2/3 cup instant milk powder
- 1/4 cup sugar
- 2 large eggs, room temp
- 2/3 cup olive oil
- 1 teaspoon salt
- 1 1/3 cups warm water, slightly warmer than room temp

TOPPING
- 1/4 cup salted butter, melted
- 1/2 teaspoon garlic salt

RECIPE NOTES

- Bake long enough for the breadsticks to brown a little on the outside, this will give them the texture you remember from your favorite Italian restaurant!
- If you want, sprinkle a little parsley over the breadsticks just before serving.

BREADSTICKS

INSTRUCTIONS

1. Line 2 large baking sheets with parchment. Set aside.
2. Add all dough ingredients to the bowl of a stand mixer in order listed.
3. Mix on medium speed for 2-3 minutes. The texture should be between a thick banana bread batter and a regular wheat-based dough (**see page xii**).
4. Turn dough out onto a floured surface and roll to coat, being careful not to incorporate extra flour into the dough.
5. Divide dough into 10 equal pieces and roll each into a rope about 8 inches long.
6. Carefully transfer to the prepared baking sheets.
7. Cover loosely with plastic wrap that has been sprayed with cooking spray.
8. Allow to rise in a warm location for about 30 minutes, until breadsticks have puffed up to almost doubled in size.
9. Preheat the oven to 400°F.
10. While the oven is preheating, combine butter, and garlic salt and gently brush over breadsticks.
11. Bake for about 15 minutes, until the breadsticks are golden brown and done inside.
12. Brush with additional melted butter and sprinkle with garlic salt to taste.

BAKING TIP

WHEN SUBSTITUTING
DAIRY FREE BUTTER,
USE A HIGH
QUALITY BUTTER
SUBSTITUTE IN
STICK FORM AS IT
WILL HAVE
COMPARABLE FAT
CONTENT.

HOAGIE BUNS

◉ YIELD: 6 BUNS ◔ PREP: 20M ⧗ COOK: 25M ◔ TOTAL TIME: 2HRS

Tired of lettuce wraps or crumbly bread? You're going to LOVE these soft and easy-to-make hoagie buns! They hold together perfectly and are great for hot dogs or any kind of sandwich.

INGREDIENTS

- 3 cups gluten free flour
- 1 tablespoon instant yeast
- 1 tablespoon sugar
- 1 teaspoon salt
- 1/3 cup instant milk powder
- 1/4 cup oil
- 1 large egg, room temp
- 1 1/4 cups warm water, slightly warmer than room temp

RECIPE NOTES

- Using a hot dog pan will make beautiful, perfectly shaped buns. You'll lose a bit of that if you bake on a baking sheet.

THEREISLIFEAFTERWHEAT.COM

HOAGIE BUNS

INSTRUCTIONS

1. Combine all ingredients in the bowl of a stand mixer and mix on medium speed for 2-3 minutes. The texture should be between a thick banana bread batter and a regular wheat-based dough (**see page xii**).
2. Lightly coat your work space with additional oil and turn dough out, then roll to coat the dough with oil.
3. Divide into 6 equal pieces and roll each into a hot dog bun shape.
4. Place the shaped dough into a hot dog bun pan, or a few inches apart on a parchment lined baking sheet.
5. Cover loosely with plastic wrap and allow to rise in a warm place for 20-30 minutes until doubled in size.
6. Preheat the oven to 350°F.
7. Brush with melted butter if you want (this will help with browning) and bake for 20-25 minutes, until starting to brown and done all the way through. Note that they won't brown much.
8. Allow to cool completely before serving.
9. Like all freshly baked breads, these hot dog buns are best served fresh! You can store leftovers in a sealed plastic bag on the counter for up to 2 days, or in the freezer for longer. When you're ready to eat, just microwave for a bit to thaw/soften, or lightly toast in the oven.

THEREISLIFEAFTERWHEAT.COM

BAKING TIP

IF AT FIRST YOU DON'T SUCCEED...I WAS A BEGINNING BAKER ONCE, AND FAILED MANY TIMES! IN FACT, MY HUSBAND AND I STILL LAUGH ABOUT THE HOCKEY PUCK ROLLS I MADE SOON AFTER HIS DIAGNOSIS. IF YOUR FIRST ATTEMPTS DON'T TURN OUT, KEEP TRYING! AND REACH OUT TO ME FOR HELP IF YOU HAVE QUESTIONS. YOU GOT THIS!

HAMBURGER BUNS

⊕ YIELD: 6-8 BUNS   ◷ PREP: 20M   ⧗ COOK: 25M   ◷ TOTAL TIME: 1 1/5HRS

FINALLY a gluten free hamburger bun that is soft, bendable, and every bit as good as a regular wheat bun! The parmesan cheese adds a beautiful flavor and color that perfectly complements a good burger.

INGREDIENTS

- 3 cups gluten free flour
- 1/2 cup parmesan cheese
- 1 tablespoon instant yeast
- 1 tablespoon sugar
- 1 teaspoon onion salt
- 1 large egg, room temp
- 1/4 cup neutral tasting oil, such as avocado or canola
- 1 1/4 cup warm water, slightly warmer than room temp

RECIPE NOTES

- If you need to make this recipe dairy free, you can omit the parmesan cheese.
- A hamburger bun pan makes this recipe super easy, but it also makes large buns. If you don't have a pan or want smaller buns, just shape and bake on a cookie sheet.
- Try making sliders! Reduce the baking time by 5-15 minutes depending on the size you make them.

HAMBURGER BUNS

INSTRUCTIONS

1. In the bowl of a stand mixer, measure and add all ingredients in order and mix on medium speed for 2-3 minutes. The texture should be between a thick banana bread batter and a regular wheat-based dough (**see page xii**).
2. Coat your working surface and hands with additional oil or water and divide the dough into 6-8 equal pieces depending on the size of bun you would like.
3. Roll each piece into a ball and flatten into a hamburger bun shape, using additional water or oil if needed to keep the dough from sticking to your hands.
4. Place shaped dough in a hamburger bun pan, or on a parchment-lined baking sheet 2-3 inches apart.
5. Cover loosely with plastic wrap and allow to rise in a warm place for 30-60 minutes until about doubled in size. I use the rapid proof option on my oven.
6. When buns have risen, brush buns with melted butter or an egg wash and sprinkle with everything bagel seasoning or sesame seeds, if you want.
7. Preheat the oven to 350°F, then bake for 20-25 minutes until they begin to brown.
8. Allow to cool completely on a cooling rack before slicing.
9. These are best served immediately, but can be stored up to 2 days at room temp, or frozen for later. If they start to get crumbly after a couple days, or when thawing from the freezer, just pop in the microwave for a bit or toast lightly in the oven.

BAKING TIP

IF YOU'RE USING A SHARED KITCHEN, CONSIDER ONLY BAKING WITH GLUTEN FREE FLOUR AND BE SURE TO THOROUGHLY CLEAN ALL SURFACES AND BAKING TOOLS BEFORE MAKING SOMETHING GLUTEN FREE. IT ONLY TAKES A TINY PARTICLE OF GLUTEN TO PRODUCE A REACTION IN SOMEONE WHO HAS CELIAC DISEASE OR IS HIGHLY SENSITIVE.

HOLIDAYS

BAKING TIP

IF YOU WANT SOFT AND BUTTERY, BRUSH THE TOPS OF YOUR LOAVES OR ROLLS WITH BUTTER (OR A BUTTER SUB) AS SOON AS THEY COME OUT OF THE OVEN. IF YOU WOULD LIKE A BIT OF A CRISPY CRUST, OMIT THIS STEP.

RESURRECTION ROLLS

⚹ YIELD: 16 ROLLS   ⏱ PREP: 45M   ⌛ COOK: 30M   ⏱ TOTAL TIME: 2HRS

These Gluten Free Resurrection Rolls bake up soft and fluffy, with a hollow space inside signifying the empty tomb. Make them for Easter or any other time! They are a sweet roll, similar to gluten free cinnamon rolls.

INGREDIENTS

DOUGH

- 3 cups gluten free flour
- 1 tablespoon instant yeast
- 3 tablespoons sugar
- 1 teaspoon salt
- 1/4 teaspoon baking powder
- 1/3 cup instant milk powder
- 1/4 cup butter, softened
- 1 large egg, room temp
- 1 1/2 cups warm water, slightly warmer than room temp

MARSHMALLOW FILLING

- 1/4 cup granulated sugar
- 1/2 tablespoon cinnamon
- 1/2 teaspoon vanilla extract
- 2 tablespoons butter, melted
- 16 large marshmallows

GLAZE

- 1/3 cup powdered sugar
- 1 tablespoon whipping cream (use coconut milk if dairy free)

RECIPE NOTES

- This is a great recipe to make with kids! Mine love to help with rolling the marshmallows in butter and cinnamon sugar.
- Try your best to tightly seal the rolls before baking. If there are any holes, the marshmallow will leak out a bit.
- For easy cleanup, line your baking pan with parchment.

RESURRECTION ROLLS

INSTRUCTIONS

1. In the bowl of a stand mixer, add flour, yeast, sugar, salt, baking powder, instant milk, butter, egg, and water.
2. Mix on low until ingredients start to combine, then on medium for 3 minutes. The texture should be between a thick banana bread batter and a regular wheat-based dough (**see page xii**).
3. If it is too dry (not sticky, easily handled, or crumbly), add a tablespoon or two of water.
4. Likewise, if it is too wet (more like banana bread, not able to be formed or handled at all in the next step), add a tablespoon or two of flour.
5. Divide the dough into 2 portions.
6. Coat your surface with additional gluten free flour, turn 1 portion of the dough out, then sprinkle more flour on top. Gently turn the dough to coat the outsides in a generous amount of flour so it isn't sticky, and roll out to a 12-inch circle. slice like a pizza into 8 sections, as if you were making crescent rolls.
7. Make cinnamon sugar by whisking together cinnamon, sugar, and vanilla.

INSTRUCTIONS CONTINUED ON NEXT PAGE

RESURRECTION ROLLS

INSTRUCTIONS CONTINUED

8. Roll a marshmallow in melted butter, then in cinnamon sugar mixture, and place toward the wide end of a triangle of dough. Repeat with remaining triangles. (See photo below.)

9. Fold the wide end of the triangle over the marshmallow and roll toward the center, tucking edges as you do so. Gently form into a ball, rolling between your hands and tucking to be sure the edges are sealed as best you can.

10. Repeat with remaining dough and marshmallows.

11. Place rolls 4X4 into a well-greased 13X9 inch baking pan, brush with melted butter and additional cinnamon sugar, and cover with plastic wrap.

12. Allow to rise in a warm place for 30-60 minutes. I use the rapid rise setting on my oven.

13. When rolls are almost doubled in size, bake in a preheated 350°F oven for 25-30 minutes, until rolls are lightly brown (the color will vary based on what flour you use). The rolls should be hollow inside and not doughy at all.

14. Allow to cool for at least 15 minutes, then drizzle with glaze.

JULEKAKE

⊕YIELD: 1 LOAF ⊕PREP: 15M ⊗COOK: 45M ⊕TOTAL TIME: 2HRS

Gluten Free Julekake (pronounced Yool-eh-ka-kyeh) is a beautiful Norwegian Christmas bread studded with raisins and candied fruits with a subtle hint of cardamom. This bread is light, fluffy, and SO easy to make! If candied fruits aren't your thing, check the recipe notes for some alternatives.

INGREDIENTS

DOUGH
- 2 1/2 cups gluten free flour
- 2 1/2 teaspoons instant yeast
- 1/4 cup sugar
- 1/2 teaspoon salt
- 1/2 teaspoon cardamom
- 1/3 cup instant milk powder
- 2 large eggs, room temp
- 1/4 cup butter, room temp and cut into cubes
- 1 cup warm water, slightly warmer than room temp

FRUIT
- 1/2 cup raisins
- 1/2 cup diced gluten free candied fruit
- 1 tablespoon gluten free flour

GLAZE - optional
- 1/2 cup sifted powdered sugar
- 2 tablespoons cream

RECIPE NOTES

If you don't like candied fruit, you can substitute the candied fruit and raisins with one of the following variations:
- **White Chocolate Pecan**: ½ cup white chocolate chips + ½ cup toasted, chopped pecans
- **Cranberry Walnut**: ⅔ cup sweetened, dried cranberries + ⅓ cup chopped walnuts
- **Cranberry Orange**: ¾ cup sweetened, dried cranberries + 1 tablespoon orange zest

JULEKAKE

INSTRUCTIONS

1. Prepare a baking sheet by lining it with parchment paper.
2. In a small bowl, toss candied fruit, raisins, and 1 tablespoon flour. Set aside.
3. In the bowl of a stand mixer, combine all dough ingredients and mix on medium-low for 1-2 minutes until the dough is smooth. The texture should be between a thick banana bread batter and a regular wheat-based dough (**see page xii**).
4. Add the fruit and mix on low until evenly distributed.
5. You can spread the dough into your prepared pan and use wet hands to round it, **OR** if you want a more rustic look like you see in the photos, you can dust your countertop with a tablespoon or two of gluten free flour, lightly coat the dough with it, and shape into a round. Do not work the flour into the dough, just use it on the outside so you can shape it.
6. Cover loosely with plastic wrap and allow the dough to rise in a warm location for 30-45 minutes, until almost doubled in size.
7. Bake at 350°F for 40-50 minutes, until the top is browned and sounds hollow when you knock on it.
8. Allow loaf to cool in the pan for 15 minutes, then finish cooling completely on a wire rack.

INSTRUCTIONS CONTINUED ON NEXT PAGE

INSTRUCTIONS CONTINUED

9. Slice the bread and serve. Julekake is traditionally served with marmalade or **geitost**, which is a brown, slightly sweet goat cheese.
10. You can also prepare a simple glaze by whisking together the powdered sugar and cream, and pouring over the top of your cooled loaf. Sprinkle with additional candied fruit for garnish if you wish.
11. This bread is best served the day you bake it, but you can keep it in a plastic bag for a day or two after and serve it toasted with gietost, cream cheese, or butter. We really enjoy it toasted.
12. Once you have frozen the bread, it's best toasted or warmed in the microwave for 10-15 seconds. I don't recommend refrigeration as the bread tends to crumble easily.

CHALLAH

YIELD: 1 LOAF   PREP: 20M   COOK: 30M   TOTAL TIME: 2HRS

A rich, eggy, and slightly sweet bread traditionally served on Shabbat and major Jewish holidays. Many recipes call for a 6-strand braid, but I like to simplify with a standard 3-strand braid.

INGREDIENTS

- 4 1/2 cups gluten free flour + extra for surfaces
- 1/3 cup white sugar
- 1/2 cup instant milk powder
- 1 teaspoon salt
- 1 tablespoon instant yeast
- 2 cups warm water, slightly warmer than room temp
- 4 large egg yolks, room temp
- 2 large eggs, room temp
- 1/2 cup oil
- Additional egg for egg wash
- 1 tablespoon butter for brushing after baking

RECIPE NOTES

- Challah bread is delicious served with butter and peach or apricot jam.
- Try using the leftovers for French toast!

CHALLAH

INSTRUCTIONS

1. Line a large baking sheet with parchment paper.
2. Add all ingredients to the bowl of a stand mixer in order listed.
3. Mix on medium speed for 3 minutes. The texture should be between a thick banana bread batter and a regular wheat-based dough (**see page xii**).
4. Coat your working surface with a little oil, and turn dough out onto it, rolling to coat. Have a small cup or bowl of water nearby as you'll need to wet your hands for this next part.
5. Divide dough into 3 equal portions and roll each into ropes of equal length, wetting hands as needed.
6. Place one end of all three ropes on top of each other and pinch together.
7. Braid the ropes, then pinch together the other ends.
8. Carefully move the challah braid to the prepared baking sheet and cover loosely with plastic wrap.
9. Allow to rise in a warm location for 30-45 minutes, until about doubled in size.
10. Thoroughly whisk additional egg and gently brush it over the braided loaf, being careful not to deflate the dough. You might have some egg wash leftover, just dispose of the remainder.

INSTRUCTIONS CONTINUED ON NEXT PAGE

CHALLAH

INSTRUCTIONS CONTINUED

11. Thoroughly whisk additional egg and gently brush it over the braided loaf, being careful not to deflate the dough. You might have some egg wash leftover, just dispose of the remainder.
12. Preheat the oven to 375°F then bake the challah for 30-35 minutes until golden brown (or when the internal temperature of the bread reaches 190°F on an instant-read thermometer)
13. Remove from the oven and brush with butter. Allow to cool completely before slicing.
14. Be sure to enjoy it fresh! It is best this way. Challah also makes fantastic French toast.
15. The best way to store gluten free bread is to slice, place in a Ziploc freezer bag, remove all the air, seal, and freeze. You can then remove a slice and pop it in the toaster or microwave as you need. It might help to put pieces of wax or parchment paper between the slices so they don't stick together.
16. Once you have frozen the bread, it's best toasted or warmed in the microwave for 10-15 seconds. I don't recommend refrigeration as the bread tends to crumble easily.

GREEK NEW YEAR'S BREAD

YIELD: 1 LOAF ⬥ PREP: 15M ⬥ COOK: 40M ⬥ TOTAL TIME: 2 1/5 HRS

Vasilopita, or Greek New Year's Bread, is a slightly sweet, bread-like cake with a subtle orange flavor that is traditionally only enjoyed on New Year's Day. For a show stopping presentation, carve a simple design into the loaf before baking.

INGREDIENTS

- 3 1/2 cups gluten free flour + extra for surfaces
- 1/2 cup white sugar
- 1/2 cup instant milk powder
- 1/2 teaspoon salt
- 1 tablespoon instant yeast
- 1 2/3 cups warm water, slightly warmer than room temp
- 1 tablespoon olive oil

- 2 large eggs, plus 1 egg for egg wash, room temp
- 1 tablespoon orange zest (about 1 orange)

FOR TOPPING

- 1 large egg, room temp
- 1 teaspoon water, milk, or cream
- sesame seeds

RECIPE NOTES

- Greek New Year's bread makes a fantastic French toast! Try serving with buttermilk syrup.
- The bread is only slightly sweet. If you prefer it sweeter, you can make a simple orange glaze to drizzle over each slice before serving by whisking together 1 ¾ cups confectioners sugar, ¼ cup orange juice, 1 tablespoon orange zest, and 1 teaspoon melted, salted butter.

GREEK NEW YEAR'S BREAD

INSTRUCTIONS

1. Grease a 9-inch round cake pan generously with olive oil or butter. Set aside.
2. To make the dough, combine flour, sugar, instant milk, salt, yeast, water, eggs, and orange zest in the bowl of a stand mixer and mix on medium-low for 2 minutes.
3. Spread into the prepared cake pan and cover loosely with plastic wrap. If you want a prettier loaf, turn the dough out onto a surface that has been lightly coated with olive oil. Put some olive oil on your hands and shape the dough into a rounded disc the size of your cake pan, then gently transfer into your pan.
4. Allow to rise in a warm location until doubled in size.
5. If you want, using a sharp knife, carve a simple design about 1/4-inch deep into the top of the loaf. Try a few swirling lines or leaves! You can skip this part if you don't want to bother with it.
6. Make the egg wash by whisking together the egg and water, milk, or cream. Using a pastry brush, brush the top of the cake and sprinkle with sesame seeds.
7. Bake at 375°F for 10 minutes, then turn the temperature down to 350°F and bake for another 30 minutes or until the top is a deep chestnut brown.
8. Allow bread to cool in the pan for 10 minutes, then transfer to a cooling rack.
9. Cool completely before slicing into wedges.

BAKING TIP

CONSIDER GETTING AN OVEN THERMOMETER TO MAKE SURE YOUR OVEN IS BAKING AT THE RIGHT TEMP, ESPECIALLY IF YOU CONSISTENTLY FIND THAT BAKED GOODS AREN'T TURNING OUT THE WAY YOU WOULD LIKE.

PUMPKIN CINNAMON ROLLS

🌱 YIELD: 8 ROLLS   🕐 PREP: 25M   ⧗ COOK: 20M   🕐 TOTAL TIME: 2HRS

These cinnamon rolls feature a pumpkin dough with browned butter, cinnamon filling, and a maple glaze. Perfect for fall or, if you're like me, any time of year!

INGREDIENTS

DOUGH

- 2 1/2 cups gluten free flour + more for rolling (gfJules)
- 1/3 cup instant milk powder
- 1/4 cup sugar
- 1 1/2 teaspoons instant yeast
- 1/2 teaspoon salt
- 1 1/4 teaspoons pumpkin pie spice
- 1 cup warm water, slightly warmer than room temp
- 1/4 cup neutral tasting oil
- 2/3 cup pumpkin puree

FILLING

- 1/4 cup salted butter
- 1/4 cup sugar
- 1/4 cup brown sugar
- 3/4 teaspoon cinnamon
- 1/3 cup finely chopped pecans *optional*

FROSTING

- 4 oz. cream cheese, room temp
- 2 tablespoons salted butter, softened
- 1/4 pound (about a cup) powdered sugar
- 1 tablespoon milk or cream + additional as needed
- 1/4 teaspoon maple extract *optional*

RECIPE NOTES

- An 8-inch cake pan won't allow for as much of a rise. Try to use a 9-inch cake pan, if you have one.
- If the filling solidifies while you're making and rolling out the dough, pop it in the microwave for 5-10 seconds to soften.

PUMPKIN CINNAMON ROLLS

INSTRUCTIONS

FOR THE FILLING

1. Brown the butter by heating it in a small saucepan over medium heat. Stir continuously for 5-8 minutes. The butter will become foamy, then you will see brown bits start to form on the bottom of the pan and smell a nutty aroma. Immediately take the pan off the stove and allow it to cool slightly.
2. Add sugars and cinnamon (and pecans if you're using them) and stir or whisk until combined. Set aside.

FOR THE DOUGH

1. Add all dough ingredients to the bowl of a stand mixer in order listed.
2. Mix on medium speed for 2-3 minutes. The texture should be between a thick banana bread batter and a regular wheat-based dough (**see page xii**).
3. Turn dough out onto a floured surface and roll to coat, being careful not to incorporate extra flour into the dough. Make sure there is enough flour on the counter to prevent the dough from sticking as you roll it.
4. Roll out the dough into a rectangle about 1/2-inch thick.
5. Using your hands (trust me, it's easiest this way), gently spread the filling mixture onto the dough. Be sure to go all the way to the edges.

INSTRUCTIONS CONTINUED ON NEXT PAGE

PUMPKIN CINNAMON ROLLS

INSTRUCTIONS CONTINUED

6. Starting at the long side, gently and tightly roll the dough, sealing as you go. If the dough sticks, use a dough scraper or spatula and a little extra flour to scrape the dough off the counter.
7. When you have finished rolling the dough, firmly seal the seam.
8. Use floss, a sharp knife, or a dough scraper to slice the roll into 8 equal pieces.
9. Place one piece in the middle of a 9-inch round cake pan that has been thoroughly greased with butter or cooking spray. Place the rest of the rolls around the center.
10. Cover with plastic wrap that has been sprayed with cooking spray and allow to rise in a warm location for 30-45 minutes, until about doubled in size.
11. Bake at 350°F for 20-25 minutes.
12. Allow to cool completely before frosting.

FOR FROSTING
1. Cream butter and cream cheese together until smooth.
2. Add remaining ingredients and mix just until smooth.

Made in the USA
Las Vegas, NV
20 December 2023

83355418R00095